Pioneering Advances for AI Driverless Cars

Practical Innovations in
Artificial Intelligence and Machine Learning

Dr. Lance B. Eliot, MBA, PhD

DEDICATION

To my incredible daughter, Lauren, and my incredible son, Michael.

Forest fortuna adiuvat (from the Latin; good fortune favors the brave).

CONTENTS

Lance B. Eliot

ACKNOWLEDGMENTS

I have been the beneficiary of advice and counsel by many friends, colleagues, family, investors, and many others. I want to thank everyone that has aided me throughout my career. I write from the heart and the head, having experienced first-hand what it means to have others around you that support you during the good times and the tough times.

To Warren Bennis, one of my doctoral advisors and ultimately a colleague, I offer my deepest thanks and appreciation, especially for his calm and insightful wisdom and support.

To Mark Stevens and his generous efforts toward funding and supporting the USC Stevens Center for Innovation.

To Lloyd Greif and the USC Lloyd Greif Center for Entrepreneurial Studies for their ongoing encouragement of founders and entrepreneurs.

To Peter Drucker, William Wang, Aaron Levie, Peter Kim, Jon Kraft, Cindy Crawford, Jenny Ming, Steve Milligan, Chis Underwood, Frank Gehry, Buzz Aldrin, Steve Forbes, Bill Thompson, Dave Dillon, Alan Fuerstman, Larry Ellison, Jim Sinegal, John Sperling, Mark Stevenson, Anand Nallathambi, Thomas Barrack, Jr., and many other innovators and leaders that I have met and gained mightily from doing so.

Thanks to Ed Trainor, Kevin Anderson, James Hickey, Wendell Jones, Ken Harris, DuWayne Peterson, Mike Brown, Jim Thornton, Abhi Beniwal, Al Biland, John Nomura, Eliot Weinman, John Desmond, and many others for their unwavering support during my career.

And most of all thanks as always to Michael and Lauren, for their ongoing support and for having seen me writing and heard much of this material during the many months involved in writing it. To their patience and willingness to listen.

INTRODUCTION

This is a book that provides the newest innovations and the latest Artificial Intelligence (AI) advances about the emerging nature of AI-based autonomous self-driving driverless cars. Via recent advances in Artificial Intelligence (AI) and Machine Learning (ML), we are nearing the day when vehicles can control themselves and will not require and nor rely upon human intervention to perform their driving tasks (or, that <u>allow</u> for human intervention, but only *require* human intervention in very limited ways).

Similar to my other related books, which I describe in a moment and list the chapters in the Appendix A of this book, I am particularly focused on those advances that pertain to self-driving cars. The phrase "autonomous vehicles" is often used to refer to any kind of vehicle, whether it is ground-based or in the air or sea, and whether it is a cargo hauling trailer truck or a conventional passenger car. Though the aspects described in this book are certainly applicable to all kinds of autonomous vehicles, I am focused more so here on cars.

Indeed, I am especially known for my role in aiding the advancement of self-driving cars, serving currently as the Executive Director of the Cybernetic Self-Driving Cars Institute.. In addition to writing software, designing and developing systems and software for self-driving cars, I also speak and write quite a bit about the topic. This book is a collection of some of my more advanced essays. For those of you that might have seen my essays posted elsewhere, I have updated them and integrated them into this book as one handy cohesive package.

You might be interested in companion books that I have written that provide additional key innovations and fundamentals about self-driving cars. Those books are entitled **"Introduction to Driverless Self-Driving Cars,"** **"Advances in AI and Autonomous Vehicles: Cybernetic Self-Driving Cars," "Self-Driving Cars: "The Mother of All AI Projects," "Innovation and Thought Leadership on Self-Driving Driverless Cars," "New Advances in AI Autonomous Driverless Self-Driving Cars,"** and **"Autonomous Vehicle Driverless Self-Driving Cars and**

Artificial Intelligence" and **"Transformative Artificial Intelligence Driverless Self-Driving Cars,"** and **"Disruptive Artificial Intelligence and Driverless Self-Driving Cars,** and **"State-of-the-Art AI Driverless Self-Driving Cars,"** and **"Top Trends in AI Self-Driving Cars,"** and **"AI Innovations and Self-Driving Cars,"** **"Crucial Advances for AI Driverless Cars,"** and **"Sociotechnical Insights and AI Driverless Cars"** (they are all available via Amazon). See Appendix A of this herein book to see a listing of the chapters covered in those three books.

For the introduction here to this book, I am going to borrow my introduction from those companion books, since it does a good job of laying out the landscape of self-driving cars and my overall viewpoints on the topic. The remainder of the book is all new material that does not appear in the companion books.

INTRODUCTION TO SELF-DRIVING CARS

This is a book about self-driving cars. Someday in the future, we'll all have self-driving cars and this book will perhaps seem antiquated, but right now, we are at the forefront of the self-driving car wave. Daily news bombards us with flashes of new announcements by one car maker or another and leaves the impression that within the next few weeks or maybe months that the self-driving car will be here. A casual non-technical reader would assume from these news flashes that in fact we must be on the cusp of a true self-driving car.

Here's a real news flash: We are still quite a distance from having a true self-driving car. It is years to go before we get there.

Why is that? Because a true self-driving car is akin to a moonshot. In the same manner that getting us to the moon was an incredible feat, likewise can it be said for achieving a true self-driving car. Anybody that suggests or even brashly states that the true self-driving car is nearly here should be viewed with great skepticism. Indeed, you'll see that I often tend to use the word "hogwash" or "crock" when I assess much of the decidedly *fake news* about self-driving cars. Those of us on the inside know that what is often reported to the outside is malarkey. Few of the insiders are willing to say so. I have no such hesitation.

Indeed, I've been writing a popular blog post about self-driving cars and hitting hard on those that try to wave their hands and pretend that we are on the imminent verge of true self-driving cars. For many years, I've been known as the AI Insider. Besides writing about AI, I also develop AI software. I do what I describe. It also gives me insights into what others that are doing AI are really doing versus what it is said they are doing.

Many faithful readers had asked me to pull together my insightful short essays and put them into another book, which you are now holding in your hands.

For those of you that have been reading my essays over the years, this collection not only puts them together into one handy package, I also updated the essays and added new material. For those of you that are new to the topic of self-driving cars and AI, I hope you find these essays approachable and informative. I also tend to have a writing style with a bit of a voice, and so you'll see that I am times have a wry sense of humor and also like to poke at conformity.

As a former professor and founder of an AI research lab, I for many years wrote in the formal language of academic writing. I published in referred journals and served as an editor for several AI journals. This writing here is not of the nature, and I have adopted a different and more informal style for these essays. That being said, I also do mention from time-to-time more rigorous material on AI and encourage you all to dig into those deeper and more formal materials if so interested.

I am also an AI practitioner. This means that I write AI software for a living. Currently, I head-up the Cybernetics Self-Driving Car Institute, where we are developing AI software for self-driving cars. I am excited to also report that my son, also a software engineer, heads-up our Cybernetics Self-Driving Car Lab. What I have helped to start, and for which he is an integral part, ultimately he will carry long into the future after I have retired. My daughter, a marketing whiz, also is integral to our efforts as head of our Marketing group. She too will carry forward the legacy now being formulated.

For those of you that are reading this book and have a penchant for writing code, you might consider taking a look at the open source code available for self-driving cars. This is a handy place to start learning how to develop AI for self-driving cars. There are also many new educational courses spring forth.

There is a growing body of those wanting to learn about and develop self-driving cars, and a growing body of colleges, labs, and other avenues by which you can learn about self-driving cars.

This book will provide a foundation of aspects that I think will get you ready for those kinds of more advanced training opportunities. If you've already taken those classes, you'll likely find these essays especially interesting as they offer a perspective that I am betting few other instructors or faculty offered to you. These are challenging essays that ask you to think beyond the conventional about self-driving cars.

THE MOTHER OF ALL AI PROJECTS

In June 2017, Apple CEO Tim Cook came out and finally admitted that Apple has been working on a self-driving car. As you'll see in my essays, Apple was enmeshed in secrecy about their self-driving car efforts. We have only been able to read the tea leaves and guess at what Apple has been up to. The notion of an iCar has been floating for quite a while, and self-driving engineers and researchers have been signing tight-lipped Non-Disclosure Agreements (NDA's) to work on projects at Apple that were as shrouded in mystery as any military invasion plans might be.

Tim Cook said something that many others in the Artificial Intelligence (AI) field have been saying, namely, the creation of a self-driving car has got to be the mother of all AI projects. In other words, it is in fact a tremendous moonshot for AI. If a self-driving car can be crafted and the AI works as we hope, it means that we have made incredible strides with AI and that therefore it opens many other worlds of potential breakthrough accomplishments that AI can solve.

Is this hyperbole? Am I just trying to make AI seem like a miracle worker and so provide self-aggrandizing statements for those of us writing the AI software for self-driving cars? No, it is not hyperbole. Developing a true self-driving car is really, really, really hard to do. Let me take a moment to explain why. As a side note, I realize that the Apple CEO is known for at times uttering hyperbole, and he had previously said for example that the year 2012 was "the mother of all years," and he had said that the release of iOS 10 was "the mother of all releases" – all of which does suggest he likes to use the handy "mother of" expression. But, I assure you, in terms of true self-driving cars, he has hit the nail on the head. For sure.

When you think about a moonshot and how we got to the moon, there are some identifiable characteristics and those same aspects can be applied to creating a true self-driving car. You'll notice that I keep putting the word "true" in front of the self-driving car expression. I do so because as per my essay about the various levels of self-driving cars, there are some self-driving cars that are only somewhat of a self-driving car. The somewhat versions are ones that require a human driver to be ready to intervene. In my view, that's not a true self-driving car. A true self-driving car is one that requires no human driver intervention at all. It is a car that can entirely undertake via automation the driving task without any human driver needed. This is the essence of what is known as a Level 5 self-driving car. We are currently at the Level 2 and Level 3 mark, and not yet at Level 5.

Getting to the moon involved aspects such as having big stretch goals, incremental progress, experimentation, innovation, and so on. Let's review how this applied to the moonshot of the bygone era, and how it applies to the self-driving car moonshot of today.

Big Stretch Goal

Trying to take a human and deliver the human to the moon, and bring them back, safely, was an extremely large stretch goal at the time. No one knew whether it could be done. The technology wasn't available yet. The cost was huge. The determination would need to be fierce. Etc. To reach a Level 5 self-driving car is going to be the same. It is a big stretch goal. We can readily get to the Level 3, and we are able to see the Level 4 just up ahead, but a Level 5 is still an unknown as to if it is doable. It should eventually be doable and in the same way that we thought we'd eventually get to the moon, but when it will occur is a different story.

Incremental Progress

Getting to the moon did not happen overnight in one fell swoop. It took years and years of incremental progress to get there. Likewise for self-driving cars. Google has famously been striving to get to the Level 5, and pretty much been willing to forgo dealing with the intervening levels, but most of the other self-driving car makers are doing the incremental route. Let's get a good Level 2 and a somewhat Level 3 going. Then, let's improve the Level 3 and get a somewhat Level 4 going. Then, let's improve the Level 4 and finally arrive at a Level 5. This seems to be the prevalent way that we are going to achieve the true self-driving car.

Experimentation

You likely know that there were various experiments involved in perfecting the approach and technology to get to the moon. As per making incremental progress, we first tried to see if we could get a rocket to go into space and safety return, then put a monkey in there, then with a human, then we went all the way to the moon but didn't land, and finally we arrived at the mission that actually landed on the moon. Self-driving cars are the same way. We are doing simulations of self-driving cars. We do testing of self-driving cars on private land under controlled situations. We do testing of self-driving cars on public roadways, often having to meet regulatory requirements including for example having an engineer or equivalent in the car to take over the controls if needed. And so on. Experiments big and small are needed to figure out what works and what doesn't.

Innovation

There are already some advances in AI that are allowing us to progress toward self-driving cars. We are going to need even more advances. Innovation in all aspects of technology are going to be required to achieve a true self-driving car. By no means do we already have everything in-hand that we need to get there. Expect new inventions and new approaches, new algorithms, etc.

Setbacks

Most of the pundits are avoiding talking about potential setbacks in the progress toward self-driving cars. Getting to the moon involved many setbacks, some of which you never have heard of and were buried at the time so as to not dampen enthusiasm and funding for getting to the moon. A recurring theme in many of my included essays is that there are going to be setbacks as we try to arrive at a true self-driving car. Take a deep breath and be ready. I just hope the setbacks don't completely stop progress. I am sure that it will cause progress to alter in a manner that we've not yet seen in the self-driving car field. I liken the self-driving car of today to the excitement everyone had for Uber when it first got going. Today, we have a different view of Uber and with each passing day there are more regulations to the ride sharing business and more concerns raised. The darling child only stays a darling until finally that child acts up. It will happen the same with self-driving cars.

SELF-DRIVING CARS CHALLENGES

But what exactly makes things so hard to have a true self-driving car, you might be asking. You have seen cruise control for years and years. You've lately seen cars that can do parallel parking. You've seen YouTube videos of Tesla drivers that put their hands out the window as their car zooms along the highway, and seen to therefore be in a self-driving car. Aren't we just needing to put a few more sensors onto a car and then we'll have in-hand a true self-driving car? Nope.

Consider for a moment the nature of the driving task. We don't just let anyone at any age drive a car. Worldwide, most countries won't license a driver until the age of 18, though many do allow a learner's permit at the age of 15 or 16. Some suggest that a younger age would be physically too small to reach the controls of the car. Though this might be the case, we could easily adjust the controls to allow for younger aged and thus smaller stature. It's not their physical size that matters. It's their cognitive development that matters.

To drive a car, you need to be able to reason about the car, what the car can and cannot do. You need to know how to operate the car. You need to know about how other cars on the road drive. You need to know what is allowed in driving such as speed limits and driving within marked lanes. You need to be able to react to situations and be able to avoid getting into accidents. You need to ascertain when to hit your brakes, when to steer clear of a pedestrian, and how to keep from ramming that motorcyclist that just cut you off.

Many of us had taken courses on driving. We studied about driving and took driver training. We had to take a test and pass it to be able to drive. The point being that though most adults take the driving task for granted, and we often "mindlessly" drive our cars, there is a significant amount of cognitive effort that goes into driving a car. After a while, it becomes second nature. You don't especially think about how you drive, you just do it. But, if you watch a novice driver, say a teenager learning to drive, you suddenly realize that there is a lot more complexity to it than we seem to realize.

Furthermore, driving is a very serious task. I recall when my daughter and son first learned to drive. They are both very conscientious people. They wanted to make sure that whatever they did, they did well, and that they did not harm anyone. Every day, when you get into a car, it is probably around 4,000 pounds of hefty metal and plastics (about two tons), and it is a lethal weapon. Think about it. You drive down the street in an object that weighs two tons and with the engine it can accelerate and ram into anything you want to hit. The damage a car can inflict is very scary. Both my children were surprised that they were being given the right to maneuver this monster of a beast that could cause tremendous harm entirely by merely letting go of the steering wheel for a moment or taking your eyes off the road.

In fact, in the United States alone there are about 30,000 deaths per year by auto accidents, which is around 100 per day. Given that there are about 263 million cars in the United States, I am actually more amazed that the number of fatalities is not a lot higher. During my morning commute, I look at all the thousands of cars on the freeway around me, and I think that if all of them decided to go zombie and drive in a crazy maniac way, there would be many people dead. Somehow, incredibly, each day, most people drive relatively safely. To me, that's a miracle right there. Getting millions and millions of people to be safe and sane when behind the wheel of a two ton mobile object, it's a feat that we as a society should admire with pride.

So, hopefully you are in agreement that the driving task requires a great deal of cognition. You don't' need to be especially smart to drive a car, and we've done quite a bit to make car driving viable for even the average dolt. There isn't an IQ test that you need to take to drive a car. If you can read and write, and pass a test, you pretty much can legally drive a car. There are of course some that drive a car and are not legally permitted to do so, plus there are private areas such as farms where drivers are young, but for public roadways in the United States, you can be generally of average intelligence (or less) and be able to legally drive.

This though makes it seem like the cognitive effort must not be much. If the cognitive effort was truly hard, wouldn't we only have Einstein's that could drive a car? We have made sure to keep the driving task as simple as we can, by making the controls easy and relatively standardized, and by having roads that are relatively standardized, and so on. It is as though Disneyland has put their Autopia into the real-world, by us all as a society agreeing that roads will be a certain way, and we'll all abide by the various rules of driving.

A modest cognitive task by a human is still something that stymies AI. You certainly know that AI has been able to beat chess players and be good at other kinds of games. This type of narrow cognition is not what car driving is about. Car driving is much wider. It requires knowledge about the world, which a chess playing AI system does not need to know. The cognitive aspects of driving are on the one hand seemingly simple, but at the same time require layer upon layer of knowledge about cars, people, roads, rules, and a myriad of other "common sense" aspects. We don't have any AI systems today that have that same kind of breadth and depth of awareness and knowledge.

As revealed in my essays, the self-driving car of today is using trickery to do particular tasks. It is all very narrow in operation. Plus, it currently assumes that a human driver is ready to intervene. It is like a child that we have taught to stack blocks, but we are needed to be right there in case the child stacks them too high and they begin to fall over. AI of today is brittle, it is narrow, and it does not approach the cognitive abilities of humans. This is why the true self-driving car is somewhere out in the future.

Another aspect to the driving task is that it is not solely a mind exercise. You do need to use your senses to drive. You use your eyes a vision sensors to see the road ahead. You vision capability is like a streaming video, which your brain needs to continually analyze as you drive. Where is the road? Is there a pedestrian in the way? Is there another car ahead of you? Your senses are relying a flood of info to your brain. Self-driving cars are trying to do the same, by using cameras, radar, ultrasound, and lasers. This is an attempt at mimicking how humans have senses and sensory apparatus.

Thus, the driving task is mental and physical. You use your senses, you use your arms and legs to manipulate the controls of the car, and you use your brain to assess the sensory info and direct your limbs to act upon the controls of the car. This all happens instantly. If you've ever perhaps gotten something in your eye and only had one eye available to drive with, you suddenly realize how dependent upon vision you are. If you have a broken foot with a cast, you suddenly realize how hard it is to control the brake pedal and the accelerator. If you've taken medication and your brain is maybe sluggish, you suddenly realize how much mental strain is required to drive a car.

An AI system that plays chess only needs to be focused on playing chess. The physical aspects aren't important because usually a human moves the chess pieces or the chessboard is shown on an electronic display. Using AI for a more life-and-death task such as analyzing MRI images of patients, this again does not require physical capabilities and instead is done by examining images of bits.

Driving a car is a true life-and-death task. It is a use of AI that can easily and at any moment produce death. For those colleagues of mine that are developing this AI, as am I, we need to keep in mind the somber aspects of this. We are producing software that will have in its virtual hands the lives of the occupants of the car, and the lives of those in other nearby cars, and the lives of nearby pedestrians, etc. Chess is not usually a life-or-death matter.

Driving is all around us. Cars are everywhere. Most of today's AI applications involve only a small number of people. Or, they are behind the scenes and we as humans have other recourse if the AI messes up. AI that is driving a car at 80 miles per hour on a highway had better not mess up. The consequences are grave. Multiply this by the number of cars, if we could put magically self-driving into every car in the USA, we'd have AI running in the 263 million cars. That's a lot of AI spread around. This is AI on a massive scale that we are not doing today and that offers both promise and potential peril.

There are some that want AI for self-driving cars because they envision a world without any car accidents. They envision a world in which there is no car congestion and all cars cooperate with each other. These are wonderful utopian visions.

They are also very misleading. The adoption of self-driving cars is going to be incremental and not overnight. We cannot economically just junk all existing cars. Nor are we going to be able to affordably retrofit existing cars. It is more likely that self-driving cars will be built into new cars and that over many years of gradual replacement of existing cars that we'll see the mix of self-driving cars become substantial in the real-world.

In these essays, I have tried to offer technological insights without being overly technical in my description, and also blended the business, societal, and economic aspects too. Technologists need to consider the non-technological impacts of what they do. Non-technologists should be aware of what is being developed.

We all need to work together to collectively be prepared for the enormous disruption and transformative aspects of true self-driving cars. We all need to be involved in this mother of all AI projects.

WHAT THIS BOOK PROVIDES

What does this book provide to you? It introduces many of the key elements about self-driving cars and does so with an AI based perspective. I weave together technical and non-technical aspects, readily going from being concerned about the cognitive capabilities of the driving task and how the technology is embodying this into self-driving cars, and in the next breath I discuss the societal and economic aspects.

They are all intertwined because that's the way reality is. You cannot separate out the technology per se, and instead must consider it within the milieu of what is being invented and innovated, and do so with a mindset towards the contemporary mores and culture that shape what we are doing and what we hope to do.

WHY THIS BOOK

I wrote this book to try and bring to the public view many aspects about self-driving cars that nobody seems to be discussing.

For business leaders that are either involved in making self-driving cars or that are going to leverage self-driving cars, I hope that this book will enlighten you as to the risks involved and ways in which you should be strategizing about how to deal with those risks.

For entrepreneurs, startups and other businesses that want to enter into the self-driving car market that is emerging, I hope this book sparks your interest in doing so, and provides some sense of what might be prudent to pursue.

For researchers that study self-driving cars, I hope this book spurs your interest in the risks and safety issues of self-driving cars, and also nudges you toward conducting research on those aspects.

For students in computer science or related disciplines, I hope this book will provide you with interesting and new ideas and material, for which you might conduct research or provide some career direction insights for you.

For AI companies and high-tech companies pursuing self-driving cars, this book will hopefully broaden your view beyond just the mere coding and development needed to make self-driving cars.

For all readers, I hope that you will find the material in this book to be stimulating. Some of it will be repetitive of things you already know. But I am pretty sure that you'll also find various eureka moments whereby you'll discover a new technique or approach that you had not earlier thought of. I am also betting that there will be material that forces you to rethink some of your current practices.

I am not saying you will suddenly have an epiphany and change what you are doing. I do think though that you will reconsider or perhaps revisit what you are doing.

For anyone choosing to use this book for teaching purposes, please take a look at my suggestions for doing so, as described in the Appendix. I have found the material handy in courses that I have taught, and likewise other faculty have told me that they have found the material handy, in some cases as extended readings and in other instances as a core part of their course (depending on the nature of the class).

In my writing for this book, I have tried carefully to blend both the practitioner and the academic styles of writing. It is not as dense as is typical academic journal writing, but at the same time offers depth by going into the nuances and trade-offs of various practices.

The word "deep" is in vogue today, meaning getting deeply into a subject or topic, and so is the word "unpack" which means to tease out the underlying aspects of a subject or topic. I have sought to offer material that addresses an issue or topic by going relatively deeply into it and make sure that it is well unpacked.

Finally, in any book about AI, it is difficult to use our everyday words without having some of them be misinterpreted. Specifically, it is easy to anthropomorphize AI. When I say that an AI system "knows" something, I do not want you to construe that the AI system has sentience and "knows" in the same way that humans do. They aren't that way, as yet. I have tried to use quotes around such words from time-to-time to emphasize that the words I am using should not be misinterpreted to ascribe true human intelligence to the AI systems that we know of today. If I used quotes around all such words, the book would be very difficult to read, and so I am doing so judiciously. Please keep that in mind as you read the material, thanks.

COMPANION BOOKS

If you find this material of interest, you might want to also see my other books on self-driving cars, entitled:

1. **"Introduction to Driverless Self-Driving Cars"** by Dr. Lance Eliot

2. **"Innovation and Thought Leadership on Self-Driving Driverless Cars"** by Dr. Lance Eliot

3. **"Advances in AI and Autonomous Vehicles: Cybernetic Self-Driving Cars"** by Dr. Lance Eliot

4. *"Self-Driving Cars: The Mother of All AI Projects"* by Dr. Lance Eliot

5. **"New Advances in AI Autonomous Driverless Self-Driving Cars"** by Dr. Lance Eliot

6. **"Autonomous Vehicle Driverless Self-Driving Cars and Artificial Intelligence"** by Dr. Lance Eliot and Michael B. Eliot

7. **"Transformative Artificial Intelligence Driverless Self-Driving Cars"** by Dr. Lance Eliot

8. **"Disruptive Artificial Intelligence and Driverless Self-Driving Cars"** by Dr. Lance Eliot

9. "State-of-the-Art AI Driverless Self-Driving Cars" by Dr. Lance Eliot

10. "**Top Trends in AI Self-Driving Cars**" by Dr. Lance Eliot

11. **"AI Innovations and Self-Driving Cars"** by Dr. Lance Eliot

12. **"Crucial Advances for AI Driverless Cars"** by Dr. Lance Eliot

13. **"Sociotechnical Insights and AI Driverless Cars"** by Dr. Lance Eliot.

All of the above books are available on Amazon and at other major global booksellers.

CHAPTER 1

ELIOT FRAMEWORK FOR AI SELF-DRIVING CARS

CHAPTER 1

ELIOT FRAMEWORK FOR AI SELF-DRIVING CARS

This chapter is a core foundational aspect for understanding AI self-driving cars and I have used this same chapter in several of my other books to introduce the reader to essential elements of this field. Once you've read this chapter, you'll be prepared to read the rest of the material since the foundational essence of the components of autonomous AI driverless self-driving cars will have been established for you.

———————

When I give presentations about self-driving cars and teach classes on the topic, I have found it helpful to provide a framework around which the various key elements of self-driving cars can be understood and organized (see diagram at the end of this chapter). The framework needs to be simple enough to convey the overarching elements, but at the same time not so simple that it belies the true complexity of self-driving cars. As such, I am going to describe the framework here and try to offer in a thousand words (or more!) what the framework diagram itself intends to portray.

The core elements on the diagram are numbered for ease of reference. The numbering does not suggest any kind of prioritization of the elements. Each element is crucial. Each element has a purpose, and otherwise would not be included in the framework. For some self-driving cars, a particular element might be more important or somehow distinguished in comparison to other self-driving cars.

You could even use the framework to rate a particular self-driving car, doing so by gauging how well it performs in each of the elements of the framework. I will describe each of the elements, one at a time. After doing so, I'll discuss aspects that illustrate how the elements interact and perform during the overall effort of a self-driving car.

At the Cybernetic Self-Driving Car Institute, we use the framework to keep track of what we are working on, and how we are developing software that fills in what is needed to achieve Level 5 self-driving cars.

D-01: Sensor Capture

Let's start with the one element that often gets the most attention in the press about self-driving cars, namely, the sensory devices for a self-driving car.

On the framework, the box labeled as D-01 indicates "Sensor Capture" and refers to the processes of the self-driving car that involve collecting data from the myriad of sensors that are used for a self-driving car. The types of devices typically involved are listed, such as the use of mono cameras, stereo cameras, LIDAR devices, radar systems, ultrasonic devices, GPS, IMU, and so on.

These devices are tasked with obtaining data about the status of the self-driving car and the world around it. Some of the devices are continually providing updates, while others of the devices await an indication by the self-driving car that the device is supposed to collect data. The data might be first transformed in some fashion by the device itself, or it might instead be fed directly into the sensor capture as raw data. At that point, it might be up to the sensor capture processes to do transformations on the data. This all varies depending upon the nature of the devices being used and how the devices were designed and developed.

D-02: Sensor Fusion

Imagine that your eyeballs receive visual images, your nose receives odors, your ears receive sounds, and in essence each of your distinct sensory devices is getting some form of input. The input befits the nature of the device. Likewise, for a self-driving car, the cameras provide visual images, the radar returns radar reflections, and so on.

Each device provides the data as befits what the device does.

At some point, using the analogy to humans, you need to merge together what your eyes see, what your nose smells, what your ears hear, and piece it all together into a larger sense of what the world is all about and what is happening around you. Sensor fusion is the action of taking the singular aspects from each of the devices and putting them together into a larger puzzle.

Sensor fusion is a tough task. There are some devices that might not be working at the time of the sensor capture. Or, there might some devices that are unable to report well what they have detected. Again, using a human analogy, suppose you are in a dark room and so your eyes cannot see much. At that point, you might need to rely more so on your ears and what you hear. The same is true for a self-driving car. If the cameras are obscured due to snow and sleet, it might be that the radar can provide a greater indication of what the external conditions consist of.

In the case of a self-driving car, there can be a plethora of such sensory devices. Each is reporting what it can. Each might have its difficulties. Each might have its limitations, such as how far ahead it can detect an object. All of these limitations need to be considered during the sensor fusion task.

D-03: Virtual World Model

For humans, we presumably keep in our minds a model of the world around us when we are driving a car. In your mind, you know that the car is going at say 60 miles per hour and that you are on a freeway. You have a model in your mind that your car is surrounded by other cars, and that there are lanes to the freeway. Your model is not only based on what you can see, hear, etc., but also what you know about the nature of the world. You know that at any moment that car ahead of you can smash on its brakes, or the car behind you can ram into your car, or that the truck in the next lane might swerve into your lane.

The AI of the self-driving car needs to have a virtual world model, which it then keeps updated with whatever it is receiving from the sensor fusion, which received its input from the sensor capture and the sensory devices.

D-04: System Action Plan

By having a virtual world model, the AI of the self-driving car is able to keep track of where the car is and what is happening around the car. In addition, the AI needs to determine what to do next. Should the self-driving car hit its brakes? Should the self-driving car stay in its lane or swerve into the lane to the left? Should the self-driving car accelerate or slow down?

A system action plan needs to be prepared by the AI of the self-driving car. The action plan specifies what actions should be taken. The actions need to pertain to the status of the virtual world model. Plus, the actions need to be realizable.

This realizability means that the AI cannot just assert that the self-driving car should suddenly sprout wings and fly. Instead, the AI must be bound by whatever the self-driving car can actually do, such as coming to a halt in a distance of X feet at a speed of Y miles per hour, rather than perhaps asserting that the self-driving car come to a halt in 0 feet as though it could instantaneously come to a stop while it is in motion.

D-05: Controls Activation

The system action plan is implemented by activating the controls of the car to act according to what the plan stipulates. This might mean that the accelerator control is commanded to increase the speed of the car. Or, the steering control is commanded to turn the steering wheel 30 degrees to the left or right.

One question arises as to whether or not the controls respond as they are commanded to do. In other words, suppose the AI has commanded the accelerator to increase, but for some reason it does not do so. Or, maybe it tries to do so, but the speed of the car does not increase. The controls activation feeds back into the virtual world model, and simultaneously the virtual world model is getting updated from the sensors, the sensor capture, and the sensor fusion. This allows the AI to ascertain what has taken place as a result of the controls being commanded to take some kind of action.

By the way, please keep in mind that though the diagram seems to have a linear progression to it, the reality is that these are all aspects of the self-driving car that are happening in parallel and simultaneously. The sensors are capturing data, meanwhile the sensor fusion is taking place, meanwhile the virtual model is being updated, meanwhile the system action plan is being formulated and reformulated, meanwhile the controls are being activated.

This is the same as a human being that is driving a car. They are eyeballing the road, meanwhile they are fusing in their mind the sights, sounds, etc., meanwhile their mind is updating their model of the world around them, meanwhile they are formulating an action plan of what to do, and meanwhile they are pushing their foot onto the pedals and steering the car. In the normal course of driving a car, you are doing all of these at once. I mention this so that when you look at the diagram, you will think of the boxes as processes that are all happening at the same time, and not as though only one happens and then the next.

They are shown diagrammatically in a simplistic manner to help comprehend what is taking place. You though should also realize that they are working in parallel and simultaneous with each other. This is a tough aspect in that the inter-element communications involve latency and other aspects that must be taken into account. There can be delays in one element updating and then sharing its latest status with other elements.

D-06: Automobile & CAN

Contemporary cars use various automotive electronics and a Controller Area Network (CAN) to serve as the components that underlie the driving aspects of a car. There are Electronic Control Units (ECU's) which control subsystems of the car, such as the engine, the brakes, the doors, the windows, and so on.

The elements D-01, D-02, D-03, D-04, D-05 are layered on top of the D-06, and must be aware of the nature of what the D-06 is able to do and not do.

D-07: In-Car Commands

Humans are going to be occupants in self-driving cars. In a Level 5 self-driving car, there must be some form of communication that takes place between the humans and the self-driving car. For example, I go into a self-driving car and tell it that I want to be driven over to Disneyland, and along the way I want to stop at In-and-Out Burger. The self-driving car now parses what I've said and tries to then establish a means to carry out my wishes.

In-car commands can happen at any time during a driving journey. Though my example was about an in-car command when I first got into my self-driving car, it could be that while the self-driving car is carrying out the journey that I change my mind. Perhaps after getting stuck in traffic, I tell the self-driving car to forget about getting the burgers and just head straight over to the theme park. The self-driving car needs to be alert to in-car commands throughout the journey.

D-08: VX2 Communications

We will ultimately have self-driving cars communicating with each other, doing so via V2V (Vehicle-to-Vehicle) communications. We will also have self-driving cars that communicate with the roadways and other aspects of the transportation infrastructure, doing so via V2I (Vehicle-to-Infrastructure).

The variety of ways in which a self-driving car will be communicating with other cars and infrastructure is being called V2X, whereby the letter X means whatever else we identify as something that a car should or would want to communicate with. The V2X communications will be taking place simultaneous with everything else on the diagram, and those other elements will need to incorporate whatever it gleans from those V2X communications.

D-09: Deep Learning

The use of Deep Learning permeates all other aspects of the self-driving car. The AI of the self-driving car will be using deep learning to do a better job at the systems action plan, and at the controls activation, and at the sensor fusion, and so on.

Currently, the use of artificial neural networks is the most prevalent form of deep learning. Based on large swaths of data, the neural networks attempt to "learn" from the data and therefore direct the efforts of the self-driving car accordingly.

D-10: Tactical AI

Tactical AI is the element of dealing with the moment-to-moment driving of the self-driving car. Is the self-driving car staying in its lane of the freeway? Is the car responding appropriately to the controls commands? Are the sensory devices working?

For human drivers, the tactical equivalent can be seen when you watch a novice driver such as a teenager that is first driving. They are focused on the mechanics of the driving task, keeping their eye on the road while also trying to properly control the car.

D-11: Strategic AI

The Strategic AI aspects of a self-driving car are dealing with the larger picture of what the self-driving car is trying to do. If I had asked that the self-driving car take me to Disneyland, there is an overall journey map that needs to be kept and maintained.

There is an interaction between the Strategic AI and the Tactical AI. The Strategic AI is wanting to keep on the mission of the driving, while the Tactical AI is focused on the particulars underway in the driving effort. If the Tactical AI seems to wander away from the overarching mission, the Strategic AI wants to see why and get things back on track. If the Tactical AI realizes that there is something amiss on the self-driving car, it needs to alert the Strategic AI accordingly and have an adjustment to the overarching mission that is underway.

D-12: Self-Aware AI

Very few of the self-driving cars being developed are including a Self-Aware AI element, which we at the Cybernetic Self-Driving Car Institute believe is crucial to Level 5 self-driving cars.

The Self-Aware AI element is intended to watch over itself, in the sense that the AI is making sure that the AI is working as intended. Suppose you had a human driving a car, and they were starting to drive erratically. Hopefully, their own self-awareness would make them realize they themselves are driving poorly, such as perhaps starting to fall asleep after having been driving for hours on end. If you had a passenger in the car, they might be able to alert the driver if the driver is starting to do something amiss. This is exactly what the Self-Aware

AI element tries to do, it becomes the overseer of the AI, and tries to detect when the AI has become faulty or confused, and then find ways to overcome the issue.

D-13: Economic

The economic aspects of a self-driving car are not per se a technology aspect of a self-driving car, but the economics do indeed impact the nature of a self-driving car. For example, the cost of outfitting a self-driving car with every kind of possible sensory device is prohibitive, and so choices need to be made about which devices are used. And, for those sensory devices chosen, whether they would have a full set of features or a more limited set of features.

We are going to have self-driving cars that are at the low-end of a consumer cost point, and others at the high-end of a consumer cost point. You cannot expect that the self-driving car at the low-end is going to be as robust as the one at the high-end. I realize that many of the self-driving car pundits are acting as though all self-driving cars will be the same, but they won't be. Just like anything else, we are going to have self-driving cars that have a range of capabilities. Some will be better than others. Some will be safer than others. This is the way of the real-world, and so we need to be thinking about the economics aspects when considering the nature of self-driving cars.

D-14: Societal

This component encompasses the societal aspects of AI which also impacts the technology of self-driving cars. For example, the famous Trolley Problem involves what choices should a self-driving car make when faced with life-and-death matters. If the self-driving car is about to either hit a child standing in the roadway, or instead ram into a tree at the side of the road and possibly kill the humans in the self-driving car, which choice should be made?

We need to keep in mind the societal aspects will underlie the AI of the self-driving car. Whether we are aware of it explicitly or not, the AI will have embedded into it various societal assumptions.

D-15: Innovation

I included the notion of innovation into the framework because we can anticipate that whatever a self-driving car consists of, it will continue to be innovated over time. The self-driving cars coming out in the next several years will undoubtedly be different and less innovative than the versions that come out in ten years hence, and so on.

Framework Overall

For those of you that want to learn about self-driving cars, you can potentially pick a particular element and become specialized in that aspect. Some engineers are focusing on the sensory devices. Some engineers focus on the controls activation. And so on. There are specialties in each of the elements.

Researchers are likewise specializing in various aspects. For example, there are researchers that are using Deep Learning to see how best it can be used for sensor fusion. There are other researchers that are using Deep Learning to derive good System Action Plans. Some are studying how to develop AI for the Strategic aspects of the driving task, while others are focused on the Tactical aspects.

A well-prepared all-around software developer that is involved in self-driving cars should be familiar with all of the elements, at least to the degree that they know what each element does. This is important since whatever piece of the pie that the software developer works on, they need to be knowledgeable about what the other elements are doing.

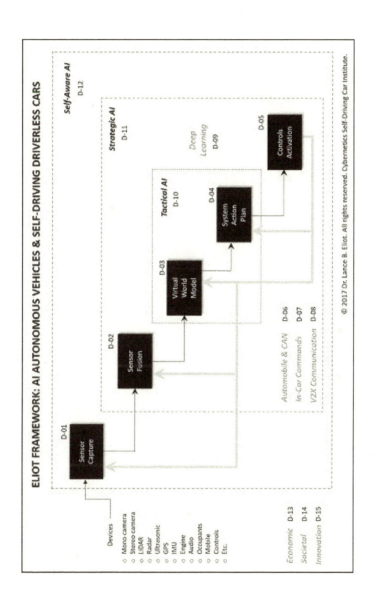

ELIOT FRAMEWORK: AI AUTONOMOUS VEHICLES & SELF-DRIVING DRIVERLESS CARS

CHAPTER 2

BOXES ON WHEELS AND AI SELF-DRIVING CARS

CHAPTER 2

BOXES ON WHEELS AND AI SELF-DRIVING CARS

Boxes on Wheels and AI Self-Driving Cars

Watch out, the rolling boxes are on their way. Many call them a box-on-wheels. That's referring to the use of AI self-driving car technology to have a vehicle that would be driverless and would deliver goods to you or more.

At the Cybernetic AI Self-Driving Car Institute, we are developing AI software for self-driving cars, and are also including into our scope the use of AI systems for boxes-on-wheels. I offer next some salient aspects about the emerging niche of boxes-on-wheels.

Let's start with a typical use case for a box-on-wheels.

You could potentially order your groceries online from your neighborhood grocer, and a little while later those groceries pull-up in front of your house as contained in a so-called box-on-wheels. You walk outside to the vehicle, enter a special PIN code or some other form of recognition, and inside are your groceries. You happily carry the grocery bags up to your apartment or house and do so without ever having to drive your car. The vehicle drives off to deliver groceries to others that have also made recent orders from that grocery store.

Notice that I mentioned that this is considered a use of AI self-driving car technology. It is not the same as what most people think of as an AI self-driving car per se. I say that because the vehicle itself does not necessarily need to look like a passenger car. A box-on-wheels can be a different shape and size than a normal passenger car, since it is not intending to carry humans. It is intended to carry goods.

If you ponder this aspect of carrying goods, you'd likely realize that it would be best to design the vehicle in a manner intended to carry goods rather than carrying humans.

Consider first what it's like to carry goods inside a passenger car. I'm sure you've tried to pile your own grocery bags into the backseat of your car or maybe on the floor just ahead of the passenger front seat. The odds are that at some point you had those bags flop over and spill their contents. If you made a quick stop by hitting the brakes of the car, it could be that you've had groceries that littered throughout your car and maybe had broken glass from a smashed milk bottle as a result. Not good.

Don't blame it on the passenger car! The passenger car is considered optimized to carry people. There are seats for people. There are armrests for people. There are areas for people to put their feet. All in all, the typical passenger car is not particularly suited to carry goods. Sure, you might place the goods into your trunk or maybe some other baggage carrying spaces of the car, but then you'd be unable to use the passenger seats in any sensible way to carry goods. Nope, don't try to make a hammer into a screwdriver. If you need a hammer, get yourself a hammer. If you need a screwdriver, get yourself a screwdriver.

Thus, I think you can understand the great value and importance of developing a vehicle optimized for carrying goods, of which it is not bound to the design of a passenger carrying car. There are a wide variety of these designs all vying to see which will be the best, or at least become more enduring, as to meeting the needs of delivering goods. Some of these vehicles are the same size as a passenger car. Some of these vehicles are much smaller than a passenger car, of which, some of those are envisioned to go on sidewalks rather than solely on the streets.

The ones that go on the sidewalks need to especially be honed to cope with pedestrians and other aspects of driving on a sidewalk, plus there often is the need to get regulatory approval in a particular area to allow a motorized vehicle to go on sidewalks. Having such a vehicle on a sidewalk can be a dicey proposition. If you are wondering why even try, the notion is that it can more readily get to harder to reach places due to its smaller size and overall footprint, and in neighborhoods where they restrict the use of full sized cars it could potentially do the delivery (such as retirement communities), even perhaps right up to the door of someone's adobe.

Some designers are going to the opposite extreme and considering boxes-on-wheels that are the size of a limo or larger. The logic is that you could store even more groceries or other goods in one that is larger in size. This could cut down on the number of trips needed to deliver some N number of goods to Y number of delivery spots. Suppose a "conventional" box-on-wheels allowed for up to 6 distinct deliveries, while the limo version could do say twelve. The box-on-wheels for the six distinct deliveries would need to come all the way back to the grocery store to fill-up the next set of six, meanwhile the limo version would have gotten all twelve put into it at the start of its journey and would be more efficient to deliver them without having to come back mid-way of the twelve.

The downside of the limo sized box-on-wheels is whether it can readily navigate the roads needed to do its delivery journey. With a larger size, it might not be able to make some tight corners or other narrow passages to reach the intended recipient of the goods. There's a trade-off between the size of the box-on-wheels and where it can potentially go.

Indeed, let's be clear that there is no one-size-fits-all solution here. There are arguments about which of the sizes will win out in the end of this evolving tryout of varying sizes and shapes of boxes-on-wheels. I am doubtful there will be only one "right size and shape" that will accommodate the myriad of needs for a boxes-on-wheels. Just as today we have varying sizes of cars and trucks, the same is likely to be true for the boxes-on-wheels.

That doesn't though suggest that all of the variants being tried today will survive. I'm sure that many of the designs of today will either morph and be revised based on what seems to function well in the real-world, or some designs will be dropped entirely, or other new designs will emerge once we see what seems to work and what does not work. It's a free-for-all right now. Large sized, mid-sized, small-sized, along with doors that open upward, downward, or swing to the side, and some with windows and others without windows, etc.

Let's consider an example of a variant being tried out today. Kroger, a major grocer, has teamed up with Nuro, an AI self-driving vehicle company, for the development of and testing of delivery vehicles that would carry groceries. The squat looking vehicle has various separated compartments to put groceries into. There are special doors that can be opened to then allow humans to access the compartments, presumably for the purposes of putting in groceries at the grocery store and then taking out the groceries when the vehicle reaches the consumer that bought the groceries.

This kind of design makes a lot of sense for the stated purpose of transporting groceries. You want to have separated compartments so that you could accommodate multiple separate orders. Maybe you ordered some groceries, and Sam that lives two blocks away also ordered groceries. Naturally, you'd not want Sam to mess around with your groceries, and likewise you shouldn't mess around with Sam's groceries. Imagine if you could indeed access other people's groceries – it could be a nightmare of accidentally taking the wrong items (intended for someone else), or accidentally crushing someone else's items (oops, flattened that loaf of bread), and maybe intentionally doing so (you've never liked Sam, so you make sure all the eggs he ordered are smashed).

There has to be also be some relatively easy way to access the compartments. Having a lockable door would be essential. The door has to swing or hinge in a manner that it would be simple to deal with and allow you access to the compartment readily and fully. You of course don't want humans to get confused trying to open or close the doors. You don't want humans to hurt themselves when opening or closing a door. The locking mechanism has to allow for an easy means of identifying the person that is rightfully going to open the door. And so on.

The locking mechanism might involve you entering a PIN code to open the door. The PIN would have been perhaps provided to you when you placed your grocery order. Or, it might be that your smartphone can activate and unlock the compartment door, using NFC or other kinds of ways to convey a special code to the box-on-wheels. It could even be facial recognition or via your eye or fingerprint recognition, though this means that only you can open the door. I say this because you might be unable to physically get to the box-on-wheels and instead have someone else aiding you, maybe you are bedridden with some ailment and have an aid in your home, and so if the lock only responds to you it would limit your allowing someone else to open it instead (possibly, you could instruct the lock via online means as to how you want it to respond).

I mention these aspects because the conventional notion is that the box-on-wheels will most likely be unattended by a human.

If you had a human attendant that was inside the vehicle, they could presumably get out of the vehicle when it reaches your home, they could open the door to the compartment that contains your groceries, and they might either hand it to you or walk it up to your door. But, if the vehicle is unattended by a human, this means that the everyday person receiving the delivery is going to have to figure out how to open the compartment door, take out the groceries, and then close the compartment door.

This seems like a simple task, but do not underestimate the ability of humans to get confused at tasks that might seem simple on the surface, and also be sympathetic towards those that might have more limited physical capabilities and cannot readily perform those physical tasks. Presumably, the compartment doors will have an automated way to open and close, rather than you needing to physically push open and push closed the compartment doors (though, not all designs are using an automated door open/close scheme).

This does bring up some facets about these boxes on wheels that you need to consider.

First, there's the aspect of having a human on-board versus not having a human on-board:

- Human attendant

- No human attendant

I've carefully phrased this to say human attendant. We don't need to have a human driver in these vehicles since the AI is supposed to be doing the driving. This though does not imply that the vehicle has to be empty of a human being in it. You might want to have a human attendant in the vehicle. The human attendant would not need to know how to drive. Indeed, even if they knew how to drive, the vehicle would most likely have no provision for a human to drive it (there'd not be any pedals or steering wheel).

Why have a human attendant, you might ask? Aren't we trying to take the human out of the equation by using the AI self-driving car technology? Well, you might want to have a human attendant for the purposes of attending to the vehicle when needed. For example, suppose the grocery carrying vehicle comes up to my house and parks at the curb in front of my house. Darned if I broke my leg in a skiing incident a few weeks ago and I cannot make my way out to the curb. Even if I could hobble to the curb, I certainly couldn't carry the grocery bags back into the house and hobble at the same time.

The friendly attendant instead leaps out of the vehicle when it reaches my curb. They come up to my door, ring the doorbell, and provide me with my grocery bags. I'm so happy that I got my groceries brought to my door and did not have to hassle going out to the vehicle. This could be true too if you were in your pajamas or maybe drunken from that wild party taking place in your home. The "last mile" of having a vehicle pull-up to your curb, or perhaps park in your driveway, or wherever, the AI self-driving car system isn't going to bridge that gap. Having a human attendant would.

Think too that the human attendant does not need to know how to drive a car and doesn't need a driver's license. Therefore, the skill set of the human attendant is quite a bit less than if you had to hire a driver. Also, the AI is doing the driving and so you don't need to worry about whether the human attendant got enough sleep last night to properly drive the box-on-wheels. Essentially, this human attendant is the equivalent of the "box boy" (or "box girl") that boxes up your groceries in the store (well, that's in stores that still do so).

Having a human attendant can be a handy "customer service" aspect. They can aid those getting a delivery, they can serve to showcase the humanness of the grocer, they can answer potential questions that the human recipient might have about the delivery, and so on. The downside is that by including the human attendant, you are adding cost to the delivery process, and you'll also need to deal with the whole aspect of hiring (and firing) of the attendants. It could make deliveries a positive thing to have a human attendant, but it can also be a negative. If the human attendant is surly to the person receiving the goods, the humanness of things could backfire on the grocery store.

Some say that the box-on-wheels should have a provision to include a human attendant, but then it would be up to the grocer to decide when to use human attendants or not. In other words, if the vehicle has no provision for a human attendant to ride on-board, the grocer then has no viable option to have the human attendant go along on the delivery. If you have the provision, you can then decide whether to deploy the human attendant or not, perhaps offering during certain hours of the day the human attendant goes along and at other times does not. Or, maybe that for an added fee, your grocery delivery will include an attendant and otherwise not.

So, why not go ahead and include a space in the box-on-wheels to accommodate a human attendant? We're back to the question of how to best design the vehicle. If you need to include an area of the vehicle that accommodates a human attendant, you then are sacrificing some of the space that could otherwise be used for the storing of the groceries. You also need to consider what must the requirements of this space consist of. For example, should it be at the front of the vehicle, akin to if the human was in the driver's seat, or can it be in the back of someplace else. You would likely need to have a window for the person to see out of. There are various environmental conditions that the vehicle design would need to incorporate for the needs of a human.

This brings up another aspect about the box-on-wheels design, namely whether it can potentially do driving in a manner that would be beyond what a human would normally do. Assuming that the groceries are well secured and packaged into the compartments, the box-on-wheels could make sharp turns and brake suddenly, if it wanted or needed to do so. If there's a human attendant on-board, those kinds of rapid maneuvers could harm the human, including perhaps some kind of whiplash or other injuries.

Also, if the box-on-wheels somehow crashes or gets into an accident, if you have a human attendant on-board there needs to be protective mechanisms for them such as air bags and seat belts, while otherwise the only danger is to the groceries. I think we'd all agree that some bumped or smashed groceries is not of much concern, while a human attendant getting injured or maybe killed is a serious matter. Thus, another reason to not have a human attendant involves the risks of injury or death to the human, which if you are simply doing grocery delivery is adding a lot of risk to the attendant and to the grocer.

Let's shift attention now to the nature of the compartments that will be housing the goods.

For the delivery of groceries, it is so far assumed that the groceries will be placed into grocery bags and that in turn those grocery bags will be placed into the compartment of the box-on-wheels. This convention of our using grocery bags goes back many years (some say that the Deubner Shopping Bag invented in 1912 was the first modernized version) and seems to be a suitable way to allow humans to cart around their groceries (rather than perhaps cardboard boxes or other such containers).

The grocery bags are quite handy in that they are something we all accept as a means of grouping together our groceries. It has a familiar look to it. Assuming that the grocery bag has some kind of straps, the manner in which you carry the grocery bag allows you to either carry it by the straps or you can carry the whole bag by picking it up from the bottom or grasping the bag in a bear hug. In that sense, the grocery bag is a simple way allowing for multiple options as to how to carry it. This is mainly important for purposes of the human recipient and how they are to remove their groceries and then transport them into their adobe.

For the moment, assume that the grocery store will indeed use a grocery bag for these purposes. You would want the grocery bag to be sturdy and not readily tear or fall apart – imagine if the box-on-wheels has no human attendant, arrives at the destination, and the human recipient pulls out their bag of groceries and it rips apart and all of their tangerines and other goods spill to the ground. The human recipient will be irked and likely not to order from that grocer again. Therefore, the odds are that the grocery bag being used for this purpose has to be as sturdy if not even more sturdy than getting a simple plastic bag or brown bag at your local grocery store.

The odds are that the grocery store will use some kind of special cloth bag or equivalent which is durable and can safely hold the groceries and be transported. Likely the grocery store would brand the bags so that it is apparent they came from the XYZ grocery store. The twist to all of this is the cost of those bags and also what happens to them. The cost is likely high enough that it adds to the cost of the delivery overall. Also, if every time you receive a delivery you get and presumably keep the bags, it means that the grocer is going to be handing out a lot of these bags over time. Suppose I get about four bags of groceries every week, and I keep the bags, thus by the end of a year I've accumulated around 200 of these grocery bags! That's a lot of grocery bags.

You might say that the human recipient should put the grocery bags back into the box-on-wheels after emptying the grocery bags of their goods.

That's a keen idea. But, you probably don't want the box-on-wheels to be sitting at the curb while the human recipient goes into their home, takes the groceries about of the bags, and then comes out to the box-on-wheels to place the empty grocery bags into it. This would be a huge delay to the box-on-wheels moving onward to deliver goods to the next person. So, this notion of the empty bag return would more likely need to be done when the human recipient gets their groceries, in that perhaps they might have leftover empty bags from a prior delivery and place those into the compartment when they remove their latest set of groceries. Then, when the box-on-wheels gets back to the grocery store, a clerk there would take out the empty grocery bags and perhaps credit the person with having returned them.

This shifts our attention then to another important facet of the box-on-wheels, namely the use of the compartments.

We've concentrated so far herein on the approach of delivering goods to someone. That's a one-way view of things. The one-way that we've assumed in this discussion is that the grocery store is delivering something to the person that ordered the groceries. The human recipient removes their groceries from the compartment and the compartment then remains empty the rest of the journey of the box-on-wheels for the deliveries it is making in this round.

Suppose though that the compartments were to be used for taking something from the person that received delivery goods. Or, maybe the compartment never had anything in it at all and arrived at the person's home to pick-up something. The pick-up might be intended to then be delivered to the grocery store. Or, it could be that the pick-up is then delivered to someone else, like say Sam. As mentioned earlier, Sam lives some blocks away from you, and perhaps you have no easy means to send over something to him, and thus you use the grocery store box-on-wheels to do so.

The possibilities seem endless. They also raise concerns. Do you really want people to put things into the compartments of the box-on-wheels? Suppose someone puts into a compartment a super stinky pair of old shoes, and it is so pungent that it mars the rest of the groceries in the other compartments? Or, suppose someone puts a can of paint in the compartment, fails to secure the lid of the paint can, and while the box-on-wheels continues its journey the paint spills all over the inside of the compartment. As you can see, allowing the recipient to put something into the compartment will be fraught with issues.

Some grocers are indicating that the recipients will not be allowed to put anything into the compartments. This is perhaps the safest rule, but it also opens the question of how to enforce it. A person might put something into a compartment anyway. They might try to trick the system into carrying something for them. Ways to try and prevent this include the use of sensors in the compartment to try and detect whether anything is in the compartment, such as by weight or by movement.

This does bring up an even more serious concern. There are some that are worried that these human unattended box-on-wheels could become a kind of joy ride for some. Imagine a teenager that "for fun" climbs into the compartment to go along for a ride. Or, maybe a jokester puts a dog into a compartment. Or, worse still, suppose someone puts their baby down into the compartment to lift out the grocery bag, and somehow forgets that they left their baby in the compartment (I know this seems inconceivable, but keep in mind there are a number of hot-car baby deaths each year, which illustrates that people can do these kinds of horrifying absent minded things).

Besides having sensors in the compartments, another possibility involves the use of cameras on the box-on-wheels.

There could be a camera inside each of the compartments, thus allowing for visual inspection of the compartment by someone remotely monitoring the box-on-wheels. You can think of this like the cameras these days that are in state-of-the-art refrigerators. Those cameras point inward into the refrigerator and you can while at work via your smartphone see what's in your refrigerator (time to buy some groceries when the only thing left is a few cans of beer!).

We can enlarge the idea of using cameras and utilize the cameras on the box-of-wheels that are there for the AI self-driving car aspects. Thus, once the box-on-wheels comes to a stop at the curb, it might be handy to still watch and see what happens after stopping. Presumably, you could see that someone is trying to put a dog into a compartment. The box-on-wheels might be outfitted with speakers and a remote operator could tell the person to not put a dog into the compartment.

The use of remote operators raises added issues to the whole concept of the delivery of the goods. You are now adding labor into the process. How many remote operators do you need? Will you allow them to actually operate the box-on-wheels, or are they solely for purposes of acting like a human attendant? There are costs involved and other facets that make this a somewhat less desirable addition to the process.

On the topic of remote operators, here's another twist for you. Suppose the box-on-wheels arrives at the destination address. Turns out that the curb is painted red and presumably the box-on-wheels cannot legally stop there. The street is jam packed with parked cars. There is no place to come to a legal stop. What should the AI of the box-on-wheels do?

We all know that a human driver would likely park temporarily at the red curb or might double-park the delivery vehicle. But, do we want the AI to act in an illegal manner? How else though will it solve the problem? You might say it needs to find a legal place to park, but that might be blocks away. You might say that people receiving the delivery will need to arrange for a legal place for the box-on-wheels to stop, but that's a pretty tall order in terms of having to change the infrastructure of the street parking and dealing with local parking regulations, etc.

Some believe that with a remote human operator you might be able to deal with this parking issue by having the remote operator decide what to do. The remote operator, using the cameras of the AI self-driving vehicle, might be able to see and discern where to park the box-on-wheels.

Would the remote operator directly control the vehicle? Some say yes, but if that's the case then the question arises as to whether they need to be licensed to drive and opens another can of worms. Some therefore would say no, and that all the remote operator can do is make suggestions to the AI of where to park ("move over to that space two cars ahead"). This though can be a kind of splitting of hairs, since it might be interpreted that a remote operator giving parking instructions is no different than themselves actually driving the vehicle.

Here's another facet to consider. How long will the box-on-wheels be at a stopped position and allow for the removal of the goods?

From the grocer viewpoint, you would want the stopped time to be the shortest possible. For every minute that the box-on-wheels sits at the curb and is waiting for the delivery to be completed, it is using up time to get to the next destination. Those further along in the delivery cycle are all waiting eagerly (or anxiously) for the box-on-wheels to get to them.

Suppose a person comes out to the box-on-wheels, opens the compartment designated for their delivery, and for whatever reason rummages around in the grocery bag, maybe doing an inspection to make sure the bag contains what they ordered. They decide to then slowly remove the bag and slowly walk up to their home and slowly put the bag inside the home. Meanwhile, they have four other bags yet to go that are sitting in the compartment. They walk out slowly to get the next bag. And so on.

If the system had calculated beforehand that it should take about four minutes to remove the bags by the recipient, it could be that this particular stop takes 20 minutes or even longer. How can you hurry along the recipient? If you had a human attendant, you'd presumably have a better chance of making the deliveries occur on a timelier basis. Without the human attendant, you could possibly use a remote human operator to urge someone to finish removing their bags. The AI system could of course also emit a reminder, having been programmed to be deal with the delivery aspects of the box-on-wheels.

This takes us to a crucial part of this discussion, namely what the AI is doing for the box-on-wheels.

The usual aspects of the AI involve the driving of the vehicle. Once the groceries are loaded into the compartments, it is given a "proceed ahead" indication at the grocery store. It then drives the vehicle to each of the destinations. At each destination, it allows for the compartments to be opened and then closed and needs to ascertain when to continue along on the journey. It could be that the closing of the compartment door is the signal that it is Okay to proceed, though as usual the AI needs to be doing some self-checks and looking around to make sure it is safe to proceed.

At the Cybernetic AI Self-Driving Car Institute, we are adding to the AI by including the aspects about the delivery aspects, which a normal AI self-driving car has no concern about and no provision for.

In essence, the typical AI self-driving car will remain dormant during the time that the box-on-wheels is stopped. All it cares about is when it should start driving again. There is no provision to communicate any further or take any other actions until it is cleared to continue driving.

Ideally, the AI would be aiding the delivery moment. This includes the detection of a human or humans that are coming to the box-on-wheels to pick-up the goods. It includes monitoring as the compartment is opened and the goods are removed. It includes monitoring as the compartment is closed. By using additional sensors on the box-on-wheels that are there for these purposes, it combines the other driving related sensors to then be involved in the delivery moment.

You can also add into this list of tasks the potential arduous parking aspects. Have you had a human driver that came to delivery something and you met them at the curb and told them to go ahead and park up ahead at the corner? I'm sure you have. The AI of the self-driving car can potentially interact with human(s) during the parking stage to help ascertain a place to pull over for the disgorging of the goods.

One other aspect about the box-on-wheels involves the kinds of goods that it is intended to carry. If there are frozen food items, you'd presumably want the compartment to be refrigerated so that the frozen items would not melt during the journey. You cannot know for sure the length of time to undertake the deliveries, given the vagaries of traffic and also the vagaries of the time during the delivery moment, and thus you can't just hope that the food will remain in proper shape during the journey. Using conventional air conditioning might not be enough to keep the food at the proper temperature.

You might be tempted to say that only certain kinds of groceries can be delivered via the box-on-wheels. Yes, you could make that constraint, but you've now made for a dilemma for the customer. If I cannot get my frozen fish and frozen pizza from the grocery store, I'll need to make my own trip there. If I am going to make my own trip there, why futz with the box-on-wheels delivery service?

This also logically takes us to another consideration about boxes-on-wheels. If true AI self-driving cars become prevalent, would I even need to use a box-on-wheels? In other words, if I owned a true AI self-driving car, which is considered a Level 5, I could just tell it to go to the grocery store and pick-up my goods. No need to use the box-on-wheels.

The counter-arguments are that not everyone is necessarily going to have a true AI self-driving car, and will be relying instead on using other people's AI self-driving cars to get around. In that sense, they might as well then use the box-on-wheels for getting their groceries. Also, even if you had your own true AI self-driving car, it might not have the refrigerated capabilities that presumably the box-on-wheels might have.

I've mentioned the idea of keeping food cold, but there's also the potential desire of keeping food hot. Perhaps from the grocery store, I order some cooked chicken that the grocery store is selling at their in-store buffet. I'd want the chicken to remain hot during the journey to me. Thus, the compartments might need refrigeration and they might also need some form of heating capability.

This also brings up the recent efforts by Domino's Pizza and by Pizza Hut to consider using AI self-driving vehicles to delivery pizza. Pizza Hut has teamed-up with Toyota and opted to try and get ovens closer to the door of the customer. These kinds of boxes-on-wheels are potentially going to either be keeping the pizza warmed-up or could possibly even be cooking the pizza during the journey of performing the delivery.

They still face the same issue about having the customer come out to the box-on-wheels to get the goods. You are having a wild party in your apartment and you've been drinking quite a bit. The pizza delivery box-on-wheels shows up outside at the curb, but there's no human attendant. You and two of your buddies stumble out the door of your place and meander to the curb, and can barely walk, let alone carry eight large pizza boxes back into the house. Not a pretty site. Things could quickly go awry. This is a conundrum for the pizza delivery business.

In the case of Domino's, they teamed-up with Ford and did an interesting experiment. They did a monthlong test in Ann Arbor, Michigan and had a human driver that was instructed to not interact with the customers at all. The vehicle contained the pizza that was to be delivered, placed in the backseat area and reachable to the customer by the vehicle rolling down the back window, and it was a pretense that there wasn't any human to interact with, thus, similar to picking up a pizza from an AI self-driving vehicle.

Some of the customers indicated they liked the idea of not having to interact with a human attendant. I can see why they might say this, having gotten pizza delivery and had to make small talk with the driver or otherwise deal with giving a tip, I've at times dreaded ordering from my local pizza place simply due to the need to interact with the delivery person.

As mentioned earlier herein, they discovered the parking problem issue of knowing where to best stop the vehicle to accommodate the customer (recall that they were pretending that the human driver could not interact with the customer – this is somewhat the case for today's AI, but in the future should not be).

One other aspect to note is the ordering of pizzas by parents for their children. Suppose you as a parent are going out for the night. You order a pizza to be delivered to the home for the kids to eat. Normally, the delivery person would come up to the door. There is some danger with this in that you are going to have the kids open the door to a stranger, but at least it is presumably someone that is "known" in the sense that they were an authorized delivery person by the pizza place.

With the advent of the box-on-wheels, the kids would need to come out to the vehicle. Depending upon the neighborhoods and other factors, I think we can all realize that this is possibly dangerous and problematic.

Boxes on wheels. There's little doubt that in spite of the potential emergence of AI self-driving cars, we'll still need some kind of specialized vehicles to do deliveries. An AI self-driving car that is optimized for carrying passengers will not be as optimized for carrying goods. This though does not mean that they cannot carry goods, and in fact we ought to expect that AI self-driving cars will indeed be carrying goods. There are some designs for AI self-driving cars that allow for a ready switchover of the interior to be for purposes of carrying people to instead carrying items.

We are still a long way away from having true AI self-driving cars. And, they will not become prevalent overnight. Thus, there is definitely an opportunity for the advent of boxes-on-wheels. There are many opportunities available in this niche and it provides an exciting source of challenges. The phrase "box on wheels" sounds perhaps demeaning to some, but it has the potential for being a money-making way to undertake deliveries, can reduce the cost of delivery, can aid society by enabling delivery, and is going in the direction of a society that wants to order online and have items delivered to them. Two cheers for box-on-wheels.

CHAPTER 3

CLOGS AND AI SELF-DRIVING CARS

CHAPTER 3

CLOGS AND
AI SELF-DRIVING CARS

When my children were young, we had a toy that they assembled consisting of seventy-five plastic interconnecting tunnel pieces, including having numerous tall ramps and winding paths, and when a marble was dropped into the topmost funnel it would be of great delight to all as we watched the marble roll throughout the structure. It was advertised as "down the tube it goes, where the marble stops, nobody knows" and presumably helped teach my children about physics (well, it was actually mainly just a lot of fun).

Being quite rambunctious, the kids sought out new ways to test the capabilities and limits of the toy. Putting one marble down the shoot was fun. Perhaps putting two marbles would be twice the fun! They tried this and it made them squeal with delight. If two marbles are twice the fun, certainly four marbles would quadruple the fun. They kept increasing the number of marbles and with each such increment the plastic contraption would shake and shimmer more so. How many marbles could the system withstand?

The kids ran to the kitchen and grabbed an empty lemonade pitcher. They then collected together as many marbles as they could find in the house. Placing the marbles into the pitcher, they envisioned that they could pour the marbles into the topmost funnel of the contraption, and by doing so would be able to flood the system with zillions of marbles (okay, I admit zillions is not quite the case, let's say at least 50 to 100 marbles, or something like that number).

My daughter and son began to jointly pour the marbles into the funnel. Sure enough, the marbles would zoom along, each following the other, doing so in a nearly continuous stream. Marble after marble, it became a blur. There were so many marbles flowing that it became difficult to watch any particular marble and instead it was a stream of them. Now we had something truly marvelous to watch. After all the marbles had been poured out of the pitcher and had made their way to the bottom of the structure, the children sat back and discussed what to try next.

They filled up the pitcher again with the marbles. They decided that rather than pouring the marbles via the spout of the pitcher and then into the funnel, they would use the top edge of the pitcher and just let the marbles all spill over into the funnel. In this manner, they could fill-up the funnel quickly, and not need to continue to hold and pour from the pitcher. They could then watch in glee as the marbles massively weaved their way throughout the system.

Holding the pitcher with their combined sets of hands, they struggled to tip it over and let the marbles blurb out into the funnel. It was a cavalcade of marbles. At first, the marbles indeed began to flow into the tunnels. But, suddenly, the marbles at the top came to a halt. Did something jam the funnel? Upon inspection, the children discovered that with so many marbles sitting in the funnel, they had collided with each other and did so in a manner that none of them was able to flow out of the funnel. Even though an individual marble could still have made its way down the funnel, the myriad of them had bunched up in a manner that prevented any single marble from proceeding.

The kids had invented a clog.

We all know about clogs in our bathroom sinks. Over time, the gunk of hair, toothpaste, and who-knows-what will inevitably cling to the walls of the pipe and prevent water from readily flowing down the pipes. You need to either use some kind of acid dissolver or a plunger or a rooter or other approach to get the gunk to break free. Clogs, I'd dare say they are universally hated and they are a pain in the neck to deal with.

There's another kind of clog that you likely have to deal with every day. If you drive to work on a freeway, which I do daily here in Southern California, there are inevitably clogs of one kind or another on the freeways here.

The first clog that I usually encounter involves navigating an on-ramp onto the freeway. For many of our freeways, we are using a metered ramp system. If you've not seen one of these before, it is a traffic signal setup on the ramp and regulates the passage of cars from the on-ramp onto the freeway. When they were first introduced in Los Angeles, some drivers hated them, while other drivers were thankful the metered system was put in place.

The way it works is that cars come from a street onto the lower part of an on-ramp and then come up to a point where there's a traffic signal on the on-ramp. When the traffic signal is green, you can proceed further onto the on-ramp and then onto the freeway. When the traffic signal is red, you are supposed to stay put until the light goes green. In some cases, the green light allows for just one car to proceed, while in other cases a posted sign states that two cars can proceed for each green light. There are some pretty hefty monetary fines for violating the traffic signal and most people tend to obey it.

During the busiest traffic times of the day, the metered light is running. When the traffic thins out on the freeway, the metered light is either shown entirely as green or they turn off the meter and it is therefore assumed that you do not need to wait and can just proceed ahead. In many cases there are actually two lanes on the on-ramp, one that is for those that can use the HOV lanes and one lane for those that aren't able to use the HOV lanes. Typically, the HOV lane is not constrained by the meter and can proceed ahead at will.

In the case of just a single lane for the on-ramp and with the meter being used, the traffic on the on-ramp is relatively orderly. Drivers wait their turn and sit on the on-ramp patiently waiting for the green (though some get irritated waiting for the green and I suppose saying they are waiting patiently is a bit of an overstatement). When the light goes momentarily green, the car at the front of the line of cars proceeds. And, if the green light allows for two cars to go at once, the second car quickly follows on the heels of the first car.

The reason why some people like this approach is that it turns what could otherwise be an ugly free-for-all into an orderly sequenced series of events. Rather than cars all jockeying for position, it is clear cut that you wait in line, in the lane, and you take your turn. It's like being in kindergarten again. Those that are worn out by line cutters and rude drivers see this as a systematic way to put them into their place and get them to act in a polite manner, whether they like it or not. The ones that hate the meters are those that feel it is an infringement of their right to drive as they wish and it seems like it takes forever for the on-ramp traffic to proceed.

A study done some years ago, around the year 2000, in Minnesota, claimed that ramp meters had a substantive positive impact on aiding freeway traffic, including that without the meters there was a 9% drop in available freeway capacity, a 22% increase in travel times, a drop in freeway speeds by 7%, and accidents increased by 26%. I'd vote you take that with a grain of salt and there are various studies that both support meters and refute the use of meters.

You might assume this metered approach eliminates any chances of a clog. Not so. There's at least one loophole in this approach when there are two lanes available via the on-ramp and when one of the lanes is the HOV one that does not need to stop for the meter.

Here's what often happens. A car at the front of the line and waiting for the meter to go green is eager to get moving, and the instant the light goes green, the car hits the gas to burst forward. Meanwhile, a car in the HOV on-ramp lane is eager to get ahead of the cars waiting for the meter, and so that driver has hit the gas to zip along past the standstill cars, doing so since they don't need to wait for a green light. You end-up with two cars both trying to rocket forward and yet the path just past the meter is often a slimming down of two lanes into one lane (the one lane that will lead onto the freeway).

Thus, you can have two cars, both of which thinks they have the right-of-way, entering into a tight squeeze of slimming down from two lanes to one lane. Sometimes, the metered driver is unaware that the HOV driver is coming up upon them. Sometimes the HOV driver doesn't realize that the metered driver is moving forward, having gotten the green light. Sometimes, both drivers know that the other driver is moving ahead and they purposely challenge each other.

If the other driver doesn't know the other one is there, they can accidently ram into each other or perhaps make a wild and dangerous swerve or similar maneuver. If both drivers know the other is there, it becomes a scary chicken match as to which one will back-down first. In fact, believe it or not, I've seen two such drivers that came to a complete halt on the upper part of the on-ramp, each not being able to proceed ahead, and each not willing to allow the other to move ahead. I've heard stories of occasions where two such drivers got out of their cars and then went to fisticuffs right there on the freeway. Road rage!

Clogs can happen in a multitude of circumstances.

A recent research study took a close look at fire ants and how they avoid creating clogs when they are developing their underground tunnel systems. The study done by researchers from the Georgia Institute of Technology, the Department of Physics at the University of Colorado Boulder, and the Max Planck Institute for the Physics of Complex Systems, involved observing ants during a collective excavation effort. The researchers placed the ants into transparent containers and rigged up a means to track them and analyze their movements. Using Lorenz curves, the researchers mathematically made various calculations about the work efforts. They proceeded to also create a simulation involving a cellular automata model and wanted to compare biological behaviors to robophysical behaviors. This work also pertains to swarm intelligence.

One of the key findings was that the ants seemed to be willing to undertake idle time for some of the ants that were outside the tunnel in order to avoid clogs in the tunnels. It was a kind of wait your turn approach. There were observed instances of ants that appeared to wait outside the tunnel and did so presumably because they were able to somehow discern that if they entered into the tunnel it would clog things up. Did the ants actually logically reach this brilliant conclusion and maybe had deeply thought through the ramifications of too many of them in the tunnel at one time? Or, was it some more innate kind of detection and reaction?

Either way that it happens, the anti-clogging method of these living creatures was fascinating to see happen and it lends additional credence to using similar kinds of strategies and tactics to be used for artificial systems such as AI based systems.

At the Cybernetic AI Self-Driving Car Institute, we are developing AI systems for self-driving cars. One aspect involves the traffic coordination of multitudes of AI self-driving cars.

There are some pundits of AI self-driving cars that seem to believe that the advent of AI self-driving cars will magically do away with any and all traffic jams. This is a rather farfetched assumption. It seems to be based on the notion that all AI self-driving cars will carefully orchestrate their collective movements and therefore they will overtly avoid any traffic jams or clogs.

If you live in some kind of utopian world, I suppose you can imagine that all AI self-driving cars will politely and carefully communicate with each other in a flawless manner and somehow arise to the challenge of being able to ensure there aren't any traffic jams. I assure you this is a thorny problem and not so easily solved.

Before launching into a discussion about the all-seeing all-knowing anti-clogging, let's also consider another factor in the advent of AI self-driving cars. It isn't going to happen overnight that we suddenly have all AI self-driving cars on our roads and no conventional cars. Right now, there are around 200+ million conventional cars in the United

States alone. Those are not going to disappear. The emergence of AI self-driving cars will occur over many years. It will take even more years for people to give up their conventional cars and gradually switch over to true AI self-driving cars, which, we don't even know yet whether people will be willing to do so.

Allow me to explain that last point about switching over to true AI self-driving cars. There are various levels of AI self-driving cars. The topmost level, Level 5, consists of an AI self-driving car that can drive entirely by the AI and does not need any human driver. In fact, the idea is that there is no provision for a human driver in a Level 5 self-driving car (the pedals aren't there, the steering wheel is not there, etc.).

Will people be willing to have only Level 5 self-driving cars for which no human driving is presumably allowed? Some people like to drive. They love to drive. They insist that driving is essentially a human right (that's a bit extreme, I realize). Those car drivers might cling to being able to drive and fight any effort to force them to no longer drive. It will be interesting to see how society and the government opt to deal with those last scrappers that won't give over to having the AI solely be the driver of cars.

The reason that their driving is important takes us back to the anti-clogging topic. The anti-clogging camp would assert that if you include human drivers onto the roadways then you are not going to achieve the full sense of anti-clogging. Those darned human drivers will inextricably cause a clog. A justification then of banning human driving would be that it would presumably then allow for no clogs. Which has the greater weight in our society, people being able to drive or eliminating traffic clogs (of course, there are other reasons for restricting or preventing human drivers)? You be the judge (for now).

For the moment, we'll sidestep the question of human drivers in the mix.

Assume that we had an all and only AI self-driving car world. Would we be able to avoid any and all clogs?

Let's use the on-ramp circumstance as an exemplar. You have AI self-driving cars trying to get onto the freeway. We can assume that the principles of HOV lane use might still apply, and so we might have AI self-driving cars that have no human occupants or maybe one human occupant that are waiting in the metered line, meanwhile there are AI self-driving cars with two or more human occupants and thus considered HOV-permitted and able to speed-up the ramp and not abide by the meter.

The meter goes green and the AI self-driving car at the head of the pack starts to move ahead. The AI self-driving car in the unfettered HOV on-ramp lane comes up to the point where the two cars are going to meet-up and needs to decide which of them goes first. This is reminiscent of the human driver problem earlier described. Now, we have AI self-driving car getting caught up in the same predicament.

What happens?

There is the presumed availability of V2V or vehicle-to-vehicle communications available. This means that the HOV on-ramp self-driving car, we'll refer to it as car "X" might initiate a V2V conversation with the AI self-driving car that was waiting for the green light, we'll refer to it as car "Q" and that X might inform Q that X is barreling ahead and please stay back.

This is somewhat akin to the fire ants. One fire ant is proceeding into the tunnel, so to speak, and the other fire ant is remaining "idle" as it waits its turn.

Here's a question for you, why should Q abide by the instructions or edict provided by X? In other words, why can't Q tell X that X should slow down and let Q proceed ahead? Why should one of them be considered the commander of the other? Indeed, some argue that our driving is based partially on a sense of "greed" or selfishness, whereby traffic generally flows because each car is doing what it can to maximize its own advantage. But, if you have two "drivers" and each of which demands to go first, what kind of tie breaker do you have?

You could say that in this case it should not be up to the two cars and their respective AI's to decide as to which goes ahead first. Instead, it should be the infrastructure. It is anticipated that our roadways will gradually be outfitted with high-tech sensors and other systems, and there will be the advent of V2I, vehicle-to-infrastructure communications.

Thus, in this example, perhaps the meter should be "smart enough" to realize that another AI self-driving car is coming up the on-ramp in the HOV lane, and so the meter then via V2I informs the Q to not proceed just yet (or, maybe keeps the red light a bit longer), and allows X to flow along through the ramp. Or, perhaps the V2I informs the X to slow down and allow the Q to proceed ahead.

How did the infrastructure determine which goes first? It could be based on some algorithm that tries to ascertain which of the two is "best" suited to go first. Or, maybe it randomly selects if otherwise everything else about the situation would be considered a tie. As an aside, if you are interested in algorithms for traffic jams solving, you might want to explore ALINEA, one of the more studied such algorithms for this purpose.

There are some that advocate we might consider implementing a points system. AI self-driving cars would earn points for certain acts and potentially need to use up points for other kinds of acts. Suppose you are human occupant in Q, and you are in hurry to get to work, you might have instructed your AI to go ahead and use up points to try and get ahead of other traffic. When in a dilemma such as the standoff at the on-ramp, perhaps the Q offers to provide points to X for purposes of letting Q go ahead. There might be a negotiation among them as to trading points for the circumstance.

It might not though still solve things because suppose that both Q and X are determined to go first, and are each willing to give up points to do so. You can include other variants such as maybe they auction points and the highest bidder wins. Etc. In any case, this can get complicated and some doubt that we'll use a point system.

A similar viewpoint is that maybe there would be electronic money exchanged. Instead of using points as a kind of barter, we might allow for the purchase of traffic maneuvers. You want onto the freeway fast, you can pay money to do so, electronically transferred in real-time (perhaps using blockchain). But, this has its downsides as it might lead to our public roadways becoming dominated by those that have money over those that do not.

So far, I've focused on the on-ramp example. This serves as a simple means to look at the clog problem.

Enlarge the scope to the freeway overall. The number of clogs and the emergence of clogs is many times the magnitude of the on-ramp example. You've got multiple lanes. Multiple on-ramps and off-ramps. Hundreds or perhaps thousands of cars. Each car is headed to its own desired location. There are miles upon miles of freeway. There are numerous freeway interchanges. Maintenance and upkeep of the freeways is taking place and can mire the roadways while doing so. And so on.

The other day, I was driving on the freeway and a car became disabled in the middle of the freeway.

Up until the point of the disabled car, the traffic had been flowing smoothly and pretty much at the maximum legal speed. The traffic began to snarl and it wasn't at first apparent as to why. As I got within a few cars of the disabled car, I could see the upcoming cars would come right up to the disabled car and then try to move into the lane to the left or right of the disabled car. The cars in those lanes would sometimes allow the other cars to get into their lane, and in other cases they would not. It's a dog eat dog world. Many drivers didn't want to allow the other cars to get ahead and wanted to preserve their own movement forward unimpeded.

I tell this story about the disabled car because you need to keep in mind that even an AI self-driving car could become disabled on the freeway. Pundits dreaming about the AI self-driving car utopia don't seem to realize that a self-driving car is still a car. A self-driving car is going suffer breakdowns. It will happen. Guaranteed.

How will the sudden disabling of an AI self-driving car while on the freeway be handled and done so in a manner that avoids any kind of clogging or traffic jam?

If the anti-clogging happens only for those AI self-driving cars near to the incident, by sharing with each other V2V, would this alleviate all clogging or would there still be some residual clogging? And, it would seem like the residual clogging would have a cascading effect. Self-driving cars downstream of the disabled self-driving car are likely to experience some impact, even if minimal.

You might suggest that there would be a master control system that would oversee all traffic. It would seek to prevent any traffic jams. Therefore, rather than the envisioned more localized P2P of the V2V, we might have a "Big Brother" kind of system to optimize traffic flow and eliminate clogs. This would seem like a rather tall task computationally, and one even questions whether it is possible to achieve, given too the logistical vagaries involved. There will also be some that find this notion somewhat repugnant as it might give the government excessive control and oversight.

It seems doubtful that a "perfect" world of no clogs is likely feasible. The goal might be instead to focus on clog minimization's and mitigation's. Overall, the hope would be to limit the severity of clogs and the prevalence of clogs. This might combine both a global master control system along with localized P2P systems. It's an interesting and challenging "edge" problem that will become more apparent as the advent of AI self-driving cars emerges. Meanwhile, I guess we'll all struggle with your day-to-day clogs, including that my kitchen sink has now clogged up and it looks like I'll need to call a plumber.

CHAPTER 4
KIDS COMMUNICATING WITH AI SELF-DRIVING CARS

CHAPTER 4

KIDS COMMUNICATING WITH AI SELF-DRIVING CARS

The duck won't quack.

Allow me to elaborate by first providing some helpful background.

Today's children are growing up conversing with a machine. The advent of Alexa and Siri has not only made life easier for adults, it also has enabled children to get into the game of talking with an automated system. These automated systems contain relatively advanced NLP (Natural Language Processing) capabilities, which many consider part of the AI umbrella of technologies. Improvements in NLP over the last decade or so has made them much less stilted and much more conversational.

That being said, we all have undoubtedly experienced the rather quick and rough edges of even today's best NLP. If you ask a straightforward question such as who is the current president of the United States, the odds are that those utterance of words can be parsed and that the context of the question can be surmised. But, if you twist around the verbs and nouns, and use slang or short-cuts in your speech, or ask a question that is not necessarily a readily factually answered query, you'll right away realize that the NLP and the AI behind it are rather limited.

I've seen senior citizens that loved interacting with today's voice processing systems and delight in the ability of the NLP to seemingly have human-like qualities. At times, people anthropomorphize the voice processing system and begin to think of it as though it is human. Generally, adults though will agree and admit that they know that the system is not a human and not truly like a human. No matter what kind of romanticizing you might do about the NLP, if you are grounded in reality you know that these systems are not able to be considered human. They for sure aren't able to pass the Turing Test.

What though about children?

Some are concerned that young children might not have the cognitive wherewithal to separate cleverly devised automation from real human interaction. Children could potentially be fooled into believing that a voice processing system is indeed a human. Suppose the voice processing system tells the child to jump up and down twenty times, would the child believe that this is the equivalent of an adult telling them to do the same thing? And, if so, are there potential dangers that a child might be instructed by a voice processing system to do something untoward and the child might do so under the belief that an "adult" is ordering them to do so?

Let's take that concern a step further. Suppose the child misunderstands the voice processing system. In other words, maybe the voice processing system said "People like to jump up and down," but what the child thought they heard was "Jump up and down" (as though it was an edict). Most adults are able to readily hear and interpret what a voice processing system says to them, but a child is bound to have a harder time with this. The child doesn't have the same contextual experience of the adult.

Now, I'm not saying that an adult will always hear and comprehend better than a child, since of course there is a possibility an adult might be failing to pay attention or otherwise can readily do a poor job of listening. I'm just pointing out that the less developed ear and comprehension of a child is prone to misunderstanding, mishearing, misinterpreting what the voice processing system might utter.

In fact, there's a whole slew of research about age-dependent acoustical and linguistic aspects of humans. Hearing words is just a small part of the processing elements. Not only do you need to hear the sounds of words, you need to be able to turn those sounds into meaning. Am I being told a statement, am I being asked a question, am I being told to do something, etc. Also, speech usually involves a dialogue between two or more parties, and thus whatever I've just heard might need to be considered in the context of the dialogue. This then involves maintaining a state of mind over time about the nature of the discussion, and it might involve problem solving skills.

These abilities to hear, interpret, understand, and respond to spoken language tend to vary over age. At very young ages of a baby, it is quite primitive. As one progresses toward young maturing years, it enhances. Presumably, once you reach adulthood, it is quite well sophisticated and honed.

When my children were babies, I used to do the usual goo-goo ga-ga with them, making baby-like sounds. People warned me that if I kept doing so, it would undermine their ability to learn language and they would be unable to speak appropriately as they grew-up. I was told that I should instead use regular speech, allowing their forming brains and minds to hone in on the nature of natural spoken language.

Studies do show that even babies are able to begin to find the pauses between spoken words and thus realize that speech consists of bursts of sounds with moments of brief silence between them. Thus, using conventional speech is a handy means for them to do their pattern matching and formulate how to find speech patterns. Admittedly, repeating to them nonsensical sounds like goo-goo isn't going to be very helpful for them when they try to learn Shakespeare.

As a side note, you'll perhaps be relieved to know that I did speak to them using regular adult language and merely sprinkled a few goo-goo's in there from time-to-time (it didn't seem to harm them and today they are fully functioning adults, I swear it!).

Part of the factor impacting children is not only the purely cognitive aspects of speech processing, but also the anatomical and physiological aspects too of their rudimentary sensory capabilities. The ears as an organ are still being developed. In a sense, they hear things differently than us adults. The pitch, duration, and formants of speech are somewhat garbled or distorted by their growing organs and body. When you look at a child, you see two ears and assume they hear things the same way you do, but that's not necessarily the case.

It is useful to consider these forms of interaction:

- Child with child
- Child with adult
- Child with AI
- Adult with AI

I've only listed a two entity style of communication, but please keep in mind that this can be enlarged to having a multitude of participants. I'm approaching herein the "simpler" case of one entity communicating to another entity. There's human-to-human communication, consisting of child with child, child with adult, and there's the human-to-machine communication, namely child with AI, adult with AI. I'll use the indication of "AI" herein to refer to any reasonably modern day NLP AI based system that does voice processing, akin to an Alexa or Siri or equivalent.

A recent research study caught my eye about young children talking to technology and it dovetailed into some work that I'm involved in. The study was done at the University of Washington and involved having children speech-interact with a tablet device while playing a "Cookie Monster's Challenge" game. When an animated duck appears on the screen, the child is supposed to tell the duck to make a quacking sound. The duck is then supposed to quack in response to the child telling it to make the quacking sound.

This seems straightforward. The twist in the study is that the researchers purposely at times did not have the animated duck respond with a quack (it made no response). A child would then need to cognitively realize that the duck had not quacked, and that it had not quacked when it presumably was supposed to do so. As an adult, you might think that maybe the duck got tired of quacking, or maybe the microphone is busted, or maybe how you told the duck to quack was incorrect, or maybe the program that animates the duck as a bug in it, and so on.

How would a child react to this scenario?

If this was a child-to-adult interaction, and suppose the adult was supposed to be saying "quack" whenever the child indicated to do so, you'd presumably get engaged in a dialogue by the child about wanting you to say the word (they were ages 3 to 5, so realize that the nature of the dialogue would be at that age level). Likewise, if it were a child-to-child interaction, one child would presumably use their natural language capabilities at that age-level to try and find out why the other child isn't responding "correctly" as per the rules of the game.

For the use of the tablet, the children tended to either use repetition, thus repeating the instruction to quack, perhaps under the notion that the tablet had not heard the instruction the first time, or would increase their volume of the instruction, again presumably under the belief that the tablet did not hear them, or would use some other such variation. The most common approach used by the children in the study was to repeatedly tell the tablet to quack (used 79% of the time). The researchers indicated that the children did not tend to get overly frustrated at this situation, and reportedly less than 25% got particularly frustrated.

The children were potentially not as familiar with using the tablet as they might be with using an Alexa or Siri (if they have one at home), and nor was the tablet presumably as interactive as an Alexa or Siri might be. Nonetheless, this study provides a spark toward exploring conversational disruptions and communication breakdowns between children and automated systems. This research was interestingly borne from a different study of another purpose that had inadvertently temporarily involved a system that became non-responsive and the children had to cope with the unintended occurrence (the researchers decided to see what would happen with intended occurrences).

What does this have to do with AI self-driving cars?

At the Cybernetic AI Self-Driving Car Institute, we are developing AI systems for self-driving cars. As part of that effort, we're keenly interested in the interaction of children with an AI self-driving car. Allow me to explain why.

Some pundits of AI self-driving cars are solely focused on adults interacting with the AI of self-driving cars. They seem to believe that only an adult will interact with the AI system. On the one hand, this seems to make sense because the thought of children interacting with the AI might be rather frightening – suppose a child tells the AI to drive the self-driving car from Los Angeles to New York City because they want to visit their favorite uncle. Would we want the AI self-driving car to blindly obey such a command and all of a sudden the self-driving car heads out for a rather lengthy journey?

I think we can all agree that there's a danger that a child might utter something untoward to the AI of a self-driving car. Let's not though assume that only a child can make seemingly oddball or untoward commands. Adults can readily do the same. If you are under the belief that an adult will always utter only the sanest and sincere of commands, well, I'd like to introduce you to the real-world. In the real-world there are going to be all kinds of wild utterances by adults to their AI self-driving cars.

In case you still nonetheless cling to the notion that adults won't do so, I'll help you to see how it could happen – suppose a drunken adult gets into an AI self-driving car and tells it what to do and where to go. Hey, you, AI, find the nearest pier and drive off the end of it, hiccup. That's something a drunken occupant could readily say. I assure you, any drunken instruction could be as nutty as a child's more innocent command or more so.

So, I'd like to emphasize that regardless of the age of the human that might be directing the AI, the AI needs to have some form of calibration and filtering so as to not blindly obey instructions that are potentially injurious, hazardous, infeasible, or unreasonable. This is not so easy to figure out. It takes some hefty NLP and AI skills to try and do this, and especially do so with aplomb.

Let's then reject the idea that children won't be interacting with the AI of a self-driving car.

Indeed, I'll give you another good reason why children are pretty much going to be interacting with the AI of the self-driving car. Suppose you decide that it's perfectly fine to send your kids to school via your shiny AI self-driving car sitting out on your driveway. The kids pile into the self-driving car and away it goes, heading to school.

I realize you are thinking that there's no need for any child interaction because you, the parent, told the AI beforehand to take your kids to school. They are now presumably having a good time inside the self-driving car and have no role or say in what the AI self-driving car does next. One of the kids it turns out ate something rotten last night and begins to toss his cookies. He yells at the AI to take him home, quickly.

What do you want to have happen?

You might say that no matter what the child utters, the AI ignores it. In this case, the AI has been instructed by you to drive those kids to school, and come heck or high water that's what it is to do. No variation, no deviation. Meanwhile, suppose the self-driving car is just a block from home and twenty minutes from school. Do you really want the AI to ignore the child entirely?

You might say that the child should call you on your smartphone, tell you they are sick, ask you to tell the AI to turn around and come home. The child then either holds the smartphone up in the air inside the self-driving car and you utter this command, or you call the self-driving car and tell it to turn around. This all assumes that you are able to electronically communicate with the self-driving car or with your child on the smartphone, and that there's no other aspects that interfere in doing so. It's not the kind of odds you probably should be betting on.

I can readily come up with reasonable scenarios wherein a child inside a self-driving car has no ready means to access an adult to provide a command to the AI and yet meanwhile the child is in a situation of some dire nature that requires providing some kind of alternative indication to the AI of where or what the self-driving car should do.

This gets even more complicated because presumably the age of the child also comes to bear. If the child is a teenager, you might allow more latitude of what kinds of instructions that they might provide to the AI. If the child is a 3-year-old, obviously you'd likely be more cautious. Some are wondering whether people are going to put their babies in an AI self-driving car and send the self-driving car on its way. This seems fraught with issues since the baby could have some form of difficulty and not be able to convey as such. I'm sure people will do this and they will at the time think it makes perfectly good sense, but from a societal perspective we'll need to ascertain whether this is a viable way to make use of an AI self-driving car or not.

I'll toss at you another reason for a child speaking to the AI of the self-driving car. Suppose that you are in the self-driving car with your 7-year-old daughter. You suddenly seize up and fall to the floor of the self-driving car. Wouldn't you want your daughter to speak to the AI and tell it that you've become incapacitated? I would think so. Wouldn't you also want your daughter to then tell the AI to take the self-driving car to the nearest hospital? I would think so.

I've had some smarmy people at my presentations on AI self-driving cars tell me that this is all easily solved by just having the adult beforehand provide a bunch of pre-recorded instructions and that the child can select only from those selections. I guess this implies that in the case of the 7-year-old daughter, you would have already anticipated that someday you might need to go to a hospital, and thus the AI would apparently say to the child that the child should pick from the following twelve options, including go to grandma's house, go to the store, go to the baseball field, go to the hospital, etc.

I'm doubtful of such an approach being very workable.

Rather than all of these fights about preventing children from interacting with the AI, I'd rather suggest that we do a better job on the AI so that it is more capable and able to interact with a child. If we had a human chauffeur driving the car, we would certainly expect that human to interact with a child in the sense of figuring out what makes sense to do and not do regarding where the car is going and how it is heading there. We ought to be aiming at the chauffeur level of NLP.

As earlier mentioned, we need to be cautious though in having the NLP seem so good that it fools the child into believing that it is truly as capable as a human chauffeur. I'd say that we are many years away from an NLP that can exhibit that kind of true interaction and "comprehension," including that it would likely require a sizable breakthrough in the AI field of common sense reasoning.

We are doing research on how children might likely interact with an AI self-driving car. Somewhat similar to the study about the quacking duck, we are aiming at having children that are supposed to be interacting with a self-driving car. What might they say to the AI? In what way should the AI respond? These are important questions for the design of the NLP of the AI for self-driving cars.

It seems useful to consider two groups of children, one that is literate in using an Alexa or Siri, and the other that is not familiar with and has never used such voice processing systems. We presuppose that those that have used an Alexa or Siri are more likely to be comfortable using such a system, and have likely already form a contextual notion of the potential limits of this kind of technology. Furthermore, such children appear to have already adapted their vocabulary to such voice processing systems.

Studies of children that regularly use an Alexa or Siri have already shown some intriguing results. Indeed, talk to the parent of such a child and you might get an earful about what is happening to their children. For example, children tend to treat Alexa or Siri in a somewhat condescending way after getting used to those systems. They will give a command or statement a question, and do so in a curt manner that they would be unlikely to do to an adult. Do this, do that, become strict orders to the system. There's no please, there's no thank you.

I realize you might argue that if the children did say please or thank you, it implies they are anthropomorphizing the system.

Some worry though that this lack of politeness and courtesy is going to spillover in the child's behavior such that it happens with other humans too. A child might begin to speak curtly and without courtesy to all humans, or maybe to certain humans that the child perceives in the same kind of role or class as the Alexa or Siri. I saw a child the other day giving orders to a waiter in a restaurant, as though the human waiter was no different than telling Alexa or Siri what is to be done.

For many of the auto makers and tech firms, they are not yet doing any substantive focused work on the role of children in AI self-driving cars.

This niche is considered an "edge" problem, meaning that they are working on other core aspects, such as getting an AI self-driving car to properly drive the car, and so the aspects of children interacting with the AI self-driving car is far further down on the list of things to do.

We consider it a vital aspect that will be integral to the success of AI self-driving cars, which, we realize is hard to see as a valid aspect right now, but once AI self-driving cars become more prevalent, it's a pretty good bet that people are going to wise up to the importance of children interacting with their AI self-driving cars.

My duck won't quack. That's something to keep in mind. You might recast the no quacking idea and say that the (inadequately designed) AI self-driving car won't talk (with children).

Restated, we need to have AI self-driving cars that can interact with children since children are going to be riding in AI self-driving cars, often without any adult in the self-driving car and without the possibility that an adult is readily otherwise reachable.

I urge more of you out there to join us in doing research on how AI systems should best to be established to interact with children in the context of a self-driving car. The AI needs to be able to jointly figure out what's best for the humans and the AI, perhaps helping to say the day, doing so in situations where children are the only ones around to communicate with. And that's no goo-goo ga-ga, I assure you.

CHAPTER 5

INCIDENT AWARENESS AND AI SELF-DRIVING CAR

CHAPTER 5

INCIDENT AWARENESS
AND AI SELF-DRIVING CARS

One of the first jobs that I took after having earned my degree in computer science involved doing work for a large manufacturer of airplanes. I was excited about the new job and eager to showcase my programming prowess. My friends that had graduated when I did were at various other companies and we were all vying to see which of us would get the juiciest project. There were some serious bragging rights to be had. The more important the project and world shaking it might be, the more you could horde it over the others of us.

My manager handed me some specs that he had put together for a program that would do data analysis. Nowadays, you'd likely use any of a myriad of handy data analysis tools to do the work required, but in those days the data analysis tools were crude, expensive, and you might as well build your own. He didn't quite tell me what the data was about and instead just indicated the types of analyses and statistics that my program would need to generate based on the data.

I slaved away at the code. I got in early and left late. I was going to show my manager that I would do whatever it took to get the thing going in the shortest amount of days that I could. I had it working pretty well and presented the program to him. He seemed pleased and told me he'd be using the program and would get back to me. After about a week, he came back and said that some changes were needed based on feedback about the program.

He also then revealed to me the nature of the data and the purpose of the effort. It had to do with the design of airplane windshields. You've probably heard stories of planes that take-off in some locales and encounter flocks of birds. The birds can potentially gum up the engines of the plane. Even more likely is that the birds might strike the windshield and fracture it or punch a hole in it. The danger to the integrity of the plane and the issues this could cause for the pilots is significant and thus worthwhile to try and design windshields to withstand such impacts.

The data that my program was analyzing consisted of two separate datasets. First, there was data collected from real windshields that in the course of flying on planes around the world had been struck by birds. Second, the company had setup a wind tunnel that contained various windshield designs and were firing clay blobs at the windshields. There was an analysis by my program of the various impacts to the windshields and also a comparison of the test ones used in the wind tunnel versus the real-world impacted ones.

I right away contacted my former college buddies and pointed out that my work was going to save lives. Via my program, there would be an opportunity to redesign windshields to best ensure that newer windshields would have the right kind of designs. Who knew that my first program out of college would have a worldwide impact, it was amazing. I also noted that whenever any of my friends were to go flying in a plane in the future, they should look at the windshield and be thinking "Lance made that happen."

Bragging rights for sure!

What happened next though dashed my delightfulness to some degree. After the windshield design team reviewed the reports produced by my program, they came back to me with some new data and some changes needed to the code. I made the changes. They looked at the new results. About two weeks later, they came back with newer data and some changes to be made to the code. No one had explained what made this data any different and nor why the code changes were needed. I assumed it was just a series of tests using the clay blobs in the wind tunnel.

Turns out that the clay blobs were not impacting the windshields in the same manner as the real-world results of birds hitting the windshields. Believe it or not, they switched to using frozen chickens instead of the clay blobs. After I had loaded that data and they reviewed the results, they determined that a frozen chicken does not have the same impact as a live bird. They then got permission to use real live chickens. That was the next set of data I received, namely, data of living chickens that had been shot out of a cannon inside a wind tunnel and that were smacking against test windshields.

When I mentioned this to my friends, some of them said that I should quit the project. It was their view that it was ethically wrong to use live chickens. I was contributing to the deaths of living animals. If I had any backbone, some of them said, I would march into my manager's office and declare that I would not stand for such a thing. I subtly pointed out that the loss of the lives of some chickens was a seemingly small price to pay for better airplane windshields that could save human lives. Plus, I noted that most of them routinely ate chicken for lunch and dinner, and so obviously those chickens had given their lives for an even less "honorable" act.

What would you have done?

While you ponder what you would have done, one salient aspect to point out is that at first I was not aware of what the project consisted of. In other words, at the beginning, I had little awareness of what my efforts were contributing toward. I was somewhat in the blind. I had assumed that it was some kind of "need to know" type of project.

You might find of idle interest that I had worked on some top security projects prior to this effort, projects that were classified, and so I had been purposely kept in the dark about the true nature of the effort. For example, I wrote a program that calculated the path of "porpoises" trying to intersect with "whales" -- my best guess was that maybe the porpoises were actually submarines and the whales were surface ships like navy destroyers or carriers (maybe that's what it was about, or maybe something completely different!).

In the case of the live chickens and the airplane windshields, upon my becoming more informed and with the realization of what I was contributing toward, presumably the added awareness gave me a chance to reflect upon the matter. Would my awareness cause me to stop working on the effort? Would my awareness taint my efforts such that I might do less work on it or be less motivated to do the work? Might I even try to somehow subvert the project, doing so under the "justified" belief that what was taking place was wrong to begin with?

When referring to how workplace related awareness can make a potential difference in worker behavior, a recent study of that phenomena gained national interest. The study examined the opioid drug crisis occurring in the United States. There are many thousands of deaths each year due to opioid overdoses and an estimated nearly 2 million Americans that are addicted to opioids. According to the study, part of the reason that opioid use has vastly increased over the last two decades is as a result of prescribing opioids for pain relief and for similar purposes.

Apparently, medical doctors had gotten used to prescribing opioids and did so without necessarily overtly considering the downsides of becoming possibly addicted to it. If a patient can be helped now by giving them opioids, it's an easy immediate solution for them. The patient is presumably then happy. The doctor is also happy because they've made the patient happy. Everyone would seem to be happy. This is not as true if you consider the longer term impacts of prescribing opioids.

The researchers wondered whether they could potentially change the behavior of the prescribing medical doctors. Via analyzing various data, the researchers were able to identify medical doctors that had patients that had suffered opioid overdoses. Dividing that set of physicians into a control group and an experimental group, the researchers arranged for those in the experimental group to receive a letter from the county medical examiner telling the medical doctor about the death and tying this matter to the overall dangers of prescribing opioids.

The result seemed to be that the medical doctors in the experimental group subsequently dispensed fewer opioids. It was asserted that the use of the awareness letters as targeted to the medical doctors was actually more effective in altering their behavior than the mere adoption of regulatory limits related to prescribing opioids. By increasing the awareness of these physicians, this added awareness apparently led to a change in their medical behavior. You can quibble about various aspects of the study, but let's go with the prevailing conclusions for now, thanks.

What does this have to do with AI self-driving cars?

At the Cybernetic AI Self-Driving Car Institute, we are developing AI systems for self-driving cars. We also remain very much aware of any incidents involving AI self-driving cars and discuss those incidents with our teams, regardless of whether those incidents relate directly to any of our work per se.

In essence, we believe that it is important for every member of the team, whether an AI developer, QA specialist, hardware engineer, project manager, and so on, for them to be aware of what's happening throughout industry about AI self-driving cars. Small incidents to big incidents, ones involving no injuries to ones involving deaths, whatever the incident might be it is considered vital to consider it.

Should the auto makers and tech firms that are also developing AI self-driving cars do likewise?

There's no written rule that says there is any obligation of the auto maker or tech firm to keep their AI developers apprised of AI self-driving car incidents. Indeed, it's often easy to ignore incidents that happen to competing AI self-driving car efforts. Those dunces, they don't know what they are doing, can sometimes be the attitude involved. Why look at what they did and figure out what went wrong, since they were not up-to-snuff anyway in terms of their AI self-driving car efforts. That's a cocky kind of attitude often prevalent among AI developers (actually, prevalent among many in high-tech that think they have the right-stuff!).

So, the question arises as to whether or not promoting awareness of AI self-driving car incidents to AI self-driving car developers would be of value to the auto makers and tech firms developing AI self-driving cars and their teams. You might say that even if you did make them aware, what difference would it make in what they are doing. Won't they just continue doing what they are already doing?

The counter-argument is that like the prescribing medical doctors, perhaps an increased awareness would change their behavior. And, you might claim that without the increased awareness there is little or no chance of changing their behavior. As the example of the chickens and the airplane windshield suggests, if you don't know what you are working on and its ramifications, it makes it harder to know that you should be concerned and possibly change course.

In the case of the opioid prescribing medical doctors, it was already ascertained that something was "wrong" about what the physicians were doing. In the case of the auto makers and tech firms that are making AI self-driving cars, you could say that there's nothing wrong with what they are doing. Thus, there's no point to increasing their awareness.

That might be true, except for the aspect that most of the AI self-driving car community would admit if pressed that they know that their AI self-driving car is going to suffer an incident someday, somehow. Even if you've so far been blessed to have nothing go awry, it's going to happen that something will go awry. There's really no avoiding it. Inextricably, inexorably, it's going to happen.

There are bound to be software bugs in your AI self-driving car system. There are bound to be hardware exigencies that will confuse or confound your AI system. There are bound to be circumstances that will arise in a driving situation that will exceed what the AI is able to cope with, and the result will at some point produce an adverse incident. The complexity of AI self-driving car systems is relatively immense and the ability to test all possibilities prior to fielding is questioned.

Furthermore, there is a perceived rush to get AI self-driving cars on our public roadways, at least by some.

The auto makers and tech firms tend to argue that the only viable means to test out AI self-driving cars is by running them on our public roadways. Simulations, they claim, can only do so much. Proving grounds, they say, are limited and there's only so much you can discover. The public roadways are the means to get us to true AI self-driving cars. The risks to the public are presumed to be worth the assumed faster pace to perfecting AI self-driving cars. You've got to accept some public pain to gain a greater public good, some say.

Are AI developers and other tech specialists involved in the making of AI self-driving cars keeping apprised of what is going on in terms of the public roadways trials and especially the incidents that occur from time-to-time?

On an anecdotal basis of asking those that I meet at industry conferences, many are so focused on their day-to-day job and the pressures to produce that they find little time or energy to keep up with the outside world per se. Indeed, at the conferences, many times they tell me that they have scooted over to the event for just a few hours and need to rush back to the office to continue their work efforts. The intense pressure by their workplace and their own internal pressure to do the development work would seem to be preoccupying them. I've mentioned before in my writings and speeches that there is a tendency for these developers to get burned out.

Here's then a proposed research project that would be interesting and informative to undertake.

Suppose that akin to the research on physicians and the awareness of opioids prescribing, we were to do a study of AI self-driving car developers and their awareness of AI self-driving car incidents. The notion would be to identify to what degree they have awareness in mind already, and whether increased awareness would aid in their efforts.

A null hypothesis could be: Developers of AI self-driving cars have no awareness of AI self-driving car incidents.

The definition of awareness could be operationalized by indicating that it consists of having read or seen information about one or more AI self-driving car incidents in the last N number of months. This hypothesis is structured in a rather stark manner by indicating "no awareness" which would presumably be easiest to break. One would assume or hope that these developers would have some amount of awareness, even if minimal, about relatively recent incidents.

The next such hypothesis could examine the degree of awareness. For example, maybe levels such as Q, R, S, and T number of impressions about incidents in the last N months, wherein we use say Q=1, R=2-4, S=5-7, T=8+, in order to indicate ranges of awareness. One potential flaw to simply using the number of impressions would be whether they are repetitive of the same incident, or another loophole is that they read or saw something but did so in a cursory way (this could be further tested by gauging how much they remembered or knew about the incident as an indicator of whether they actually gained awareness per se or not).

The next aspect to consider is whether awareness makes a difference in behavior.

In the case of the physicians and the opioids prescribing, it was indicated that their presumed increased awareness led to less prescriptions of opioids being written. We don't know for sure that the increased awareness "caused" that change in behavior, and it could be that some other factor produced the change, but in any case, the study suggests or asserts that the two aspects went hand-in-hand.

What might an AI developer do differently as a result of increased awareness about AI self-driving car incidents?

We can postulate that they might become more careful and retrospective about the AI systems they are developing. They might take longer to develop their code in the belief that they need to be more cautious to pay attention to systems safety related aspects. They might increase the amount of testing time. They might use tools for inspecting their code that they hadn't used before or might re-double their use of such tools. They might devise new safety mechanisms for their systems that they had not otherwise done previously.

They might within their firm become an advocate for greater attention and time towards AI systems safety. They might seek to collaborate more so with the QA teams or others that are tasked with trying to find bugs and errors and do other kinds of systems testing. They might seek to bolster AI safety related practices within the company. They might seek to learn more about how to improve their AI system safety skills and how to apply them to the job. They might pushback within the firm at deadlines that don't take into account prudent AI systems safety considerations. And so on.

For purposes of a research study, it would be necessary to somehow quantify those potential outcomes so as to readily measure whether the awareness does have an impact. The quantification could be subjectively based in that the developers in the study could be asked to rate their changes as based on a list of the possible kinds of changes. This is perhaps the simplest and easiest way to determine it. A more arduous and satisfying means would be to try and arrive at true counts of other signifiers of those changes.

Similar to the physicians and opioids study, there would be a control group and an experimental or treatment group. The treatment group might be provided with information about recent AI self-driving car incidents and then post-awareness a follow-up some X days or weeks later try to discern whether their behavior has changed as a result of the treatment. It would not be necessary axiomatic that any such changes in behavior could be entirely construed as due to the awareness increase, but it would seem like a reasonable inference. There is also the chance of a classic Hawthorne effect coming to play, and for which the research study would want to consider how to best handle.

AI developers for self-driving cars are dealing with systems that involve life-and-death. In the pell-mell rush to try and get AI self-driving cars onto our roadways, we all collectively need to be mindful of the dangers that a multi-ton car can have if the AI encounters difficulties and runs into other cars, or runs into pedestrians, or otherwise might lead to human injuries or deaths.

Though AI developers certainly grasp this overall perspective, in the day-to-day throes of slinging code and building Machine Learning systems for self-driving cars it can become a somewhat lost or lessened consideration, and instead the push to get things going can overtake that awareness. We believe fervently that AI developers need to keep this awareness at the forefront of their efforts, and by purposely allow time for it and structuring it as part of the job effort, it is our hope that it makes a difference in the reliability and ultimate safety of these AI systems. That's what we believe!

CHAPTER 6

EMOTION RECOGNITION
AND
AI SELF-DRIVING CARS

CHAPTER 6

EMOTION RECOGNITION

AND

AI SELF-DRIVING CARS

President Abraham Lincoln was considered an emotional person. I realize this seems counter-intuitive to what most people perceive about Lincoln's persona and reputation. He undoubtedly dealt with a lot of people that were highly emotional and had to provide a calming influence on them. We tend to think of Lincoln as someone that remained calm amidst an enormous cultural and political and societal storm in our country.

Meanwhile, he struggled with trying to rein in his own emotions. In a letter he wrote in 1841 to a congressman, Lincoln expressed that if perchance how he (Lincoln) felt was distributed to the whole human family, there would consequently not be even one cheerful face on earth.

I suspect that most of us wrestle with our emotions. It's usually an ongoing tussle. Many in the high-tech field admire the Star Trek character Mr. Spock or Data due to their ability to keep their emotions in-check. Indeed, many high-tech people try to do so themselves, of which, sometimes others then accuse them of being staid, uncaring, and unmoving. I dare say some of them would take that as a great compliment.

When referring to emotions, there are lots of varied definitions of what kinds of emotions exist. Some try to say that similar to how colors have a base set and you can then mix-and-match those base colors to render additional colors, so the same applies to emotions. They assert that there are some fundamental emotions and we then mix-and-match those to get other emotions. But, there is much disagreement about what are the core or fundamental emotions and it's generally an unsettled debate.

One viewpoint has been that there are six core emotions:

- Anger

- Disgust

- Fear

- Happiness

- Sadness

- Surprise

I'm guessing that if you closely consider those six, you'll maybe right away start to question how those six are the core. Aren't there other emotions that could also be considered core? How would those six be combined to make all of the other seemingly emotions that we have? And so on. This highlights my point about there being quite a debate on this matter.

Some claim that these emotions are also to be considered core:
- Amusement
- Awe
- Contentment
- Desire
- Embarrassment
- Pain
- Relief
- Sympathy

Some further claim these are also considered core:
- Boredom
- Confusion
- Interest
- Pride
- Shame
- Contempt
- Interest
- Relief
- Triumph

Say what? All of those are to be considered core?

You might begin to think it is just a random list of words or maybe an unending list of words. I'm sure that if you turn to a colleague and start to go through the list with them, you'll end-up in a bitter battle over which words should be considered emotions, and which are not, and also whether they belong in any "core" related list or not. Please don't go to fisticuffs over this.

Anyway, you'll find that there are various attempts at trying to pin down the lists of emotions, including charts, matrixes, and even a wheel of emotions. This brings up another salient point, namely whether emotions are universal in that all humans have them, or whether it is a culturally induced aspect and thus differs from culture to culture. Not only might there be a difference by culture, you could also potentially suggest that there are differences over time – did the primitive caveman and cavewoman have the same laundry list of emotions as we now have?

Maybe our emotions are another example of nature versus nurture. Perhaps some emotions are innate and come with our DNA. Other emotions are possibly learned. You could try to take an extreme position and suggest that all emotions are innate, or likewise the extreme posture that all emotions are learned (and none are innate). Good luck on that. It's an open question and there are lots of researchers poking and prodding at trying to solve foundational questions about emotions.

Are humans uniquely the only creatures that have emotions? At one point in time, some argued that animals cannot have emotions since they are presumably unthinking, and that only humans can feel emotions. Others say that emotions are not in our heads, but instead in our hearts, which for those that are more scientifically based they find rather incredulous because the heart is considered merely an organ for pumping blood. In that strict view, emotions must arise presumably via our minds. In any case, animals do have brains and so ultimately most would agree that they seem to exhibit emotions too.

Speaking of the notion of exhibiting emotions, it brings up another important points about emotions. Some suggest that we have internal emotions and that we also express emotions externally. You might be feeling unhappy on the inside (let's consider unhappiness to be an emotion, for purposes of discussion herein), and yet to the rest of us you appear to be expressing a happy emotion. Therefore, others that look at you might not know what your "true" emotional state is.

You might be purposely hiding or burying your true emotional state, seeking to keep it hidden from view. If you ever watch a poker tournament, you'll see the players often times wearing hoodies and sunglasses, since they are worried that a subtle look in their eye or a movement of their forehead might give away their inner emotion. They might have all aces and be eager to take the pot of money, but if you suspect they are ecstatic then you might not be bluffed into upping the ante.

This also points out that the hiding of emotions might also involve the display of emotions as a false portrayal. You might really be unhappy and intentionally displaying a smiling happy look. The smiling happy look didn't occur by happenstance. Instead, you are trying to make yourself appear to have a certain emotion, even though on the inside you don't believe you embody it. Some might say that we wear emotional masks on our faces, which at times differs with our inner emotional state.

Emotion is often characterized as occurring in a state-based manner. From moment to moment, your emotions might change. I think we've all encountered the roller coaster emotional person that at first was laughing uproariously and then a few moments later cried a torrent. It is believed that we might have an established emotional state that is our base, and then it is apt to vary depending upon the circumstances and situation.

Many might consider you to be a calm person that appears to be emotionless, and so that's the base state that you seem to be working from. We don't know if its innate or learned, but anyway its what you've seemingly established as your base state. If you suddenly have a boat anchor dropped on your foot, you could possibly leap outside of your calm base state and become irritated, upset, yelling and screaming. Those that know you would likely say that it was uncharacteristic of you. The situation though would certainly be one that we all might discern made sense that it dragged you out of your base state into a more emotionally laden one.

Your base emotional state might change over time. Maybe you had one base state as a child, another as a teenager, and yet another as an adult. It can change too for a variety of reasons, such as a person that perhaps is highly emotional and seems to wear their emotions on their sleeves, and perhaps they undergo some kind of therapy or treatment to keep better control of their emotions. They then become a less emotional driven person, at least as far as the rest of us can tell.

The advent of smartphones and the taking of selfies has led to interest in being able to discern computationally someone's emotions from how they look. Social media sites are each clamoring to add computer-based capabilities that try to discern the emotional state of someone as depicted in a picture or a video.

This kind of sentiment analysis can be very handy. If you are running an video ad for the latest new laundry detergent, and you can capture the facial reaction of someone watching the ad, it might computationally be possible to guess at how the person reacted to the ad. A smiling face might imply that they are interested in buying the soap and thus you could next offer then a discount coupon to get them to act on those emotions.

There is a grand race right now of trying to create a really good emotion detector. The most obvious way to do this involves analyzing a picture of someone's face. Are they smiling? Are they sad? Are they yelling? Are they tight lipped? These are all relatively easy aspects to scan and try to find inside a picture of someone's face. You might need to deal with difficulties such as something obscuring the face, perhaps they have a hoodie on and are wearing sunglasses, or maybe someone else was standing in front of them. This make things a bit harder and so it isn't always a slam dunk to find the emotions.

It's also important to not jump to conclusions simply due to a facial expression. You might have a facial expression that lasted for a split second, and an instant later you had a different facial expression. Does it make sense to scan the first instance and conclude something about your emotional state? Maybe not. It might be that you'd need to look at the face over a series of time shots, such as by inspecting video, rather than looking solely at a brief instant in time.

Even if you do get a clear facial expression to use, there are a variety of twists and turns in terms of interpreting emotion from a facial expression. In some cultures, the mouth that looks like it is shaped into a happy mood might actually be considered a sad look. Or, maybe the person was trying to fool the camera and so put on a fake look for a brief moment, meanwhile they really were in a quite different emotional state.

There are other telltale aspects about your emotion beyond just your facial expression. Your gestures such as waving your arms and the movement of your hands and fingers can be another vital signal of your emotional state. Your manner of speech can also express your emotions. Does your voice sound strained or is it highly confident? There are a slew of ways to try and gauge the emotional state of a human, and so you would need to tie together a variety of elements if you presumably want to get a full sense of the emotions of a person at any given point in time.

One newer avenue of keen interest involves your breathing rate. Recent studies show that by detecting how you are breathing that it can aid in revealing your emotions. Early studies examined babies to see if it was feasible to readily measure a baby's breathing and deduce its heartrate. It has become a focus now to study human micro-motions of their chest and other body areas to see if it is possible to detect via breathing the status of the human.

It is asserted that the physiological interplay of the heart, the breathing, the body, and the emotions, makes for a potent means of figuring out the emotional state of a person. Some studies suggest that there is a statistical correlation between the variants in your heartbeat intervals and your emotional state, and that the heartbeat intervals can potentially be divined by using your breathing. You should be cautioned though that the morphology of the human body comes to play here and that chest displacement and heart displacement can involve a great deal of signal-to-interference-and-noise (SINR).

At first glance, you might be thinking that using the breathing of a human to try and detect emotions is simply another example of looking at their face or gestures. What makes this added technique quite interesting is that rather than trying to figure out the breathing via a visual or audio means, it is shown that it is possible to do so via RF signals.

This means that for example you could potentially use a WiFi to figure out someone's emotional state. The WiFi is sending out signals and for which they will possibly bounce off objects such as a human and their chest. The reflections back to the WiFi device could then be used to try ascertain the movement of your chest and therefore your breathing aspects. This is a clever means of turning WiFi into a kind of radar device.

Some might view this as a scary proposition, since it implies that wherever there is WiFi setup, potentially it could "spy" on you and be trying to determine your emotional state. Well, yes, it does seem possible that this can occur. The upside is that when you come home after a long day at the office, and you enter into your house, the WiFi might be able to figure out that you've had a tough day and are emotionally distraught, and need some emotional soothing by the music being played in the house and the lighting, etc.

What does this have to do with AI self-driving cars?

At the Cybernetic AI Self-Driving Car Institute, we are developing AI systems for self-driving cars. One aspect about self-driving cars is that they are likely to be including humans inside of the cars, whether due to the human co-driving with the AI or due to the human being driven entirely by the AI.

It would be advantageous, potentially, for the AI to try and discern the emotional state of the humans that are in or around the AI self-driving car.

I realize this seems kind of spooky like a science fiction story. Nonetheless, when you consider this logically, it makes sense that the AI might be able to do a better job of the driving of the self-driving car if it could discern the emotions of the humans involved.

Suppose a human gets into an AI self-driving car and yells at the AI to take them to the nearest pier and drive off the end of it. Should the AI blindly obey this command? I think we'd all agree that the AI would be "unwise" to abide by such a command.

The AI needs to have Natural Language Processing (NLP) capabilities to parse the words being uttered by the human. The NLP needs to then be able to interpret the words and try to figure out what the human has said. In the effort of understanding the words themselves, it is helpful to also try and comprehend how the words were expressed.

I might say to you that I think Joe is a really smart guy. Did I really mean that he is smart? Or, was I perhaps saying this in a sardonic or cynical manner. It could be that I'm trying to express that Joe is really as dumb as a tree stump.

But, I've via my words said something quite different. That's the trick of our human languages and interaction. The words alone are not sufficient to determine what our meaning consists of.

I hope you can see that if we could detect the emotions of a human, it has the possibility of increasing the conversational aspects with humans in terms of what the AI can do. I'm not suggesting that the AI will always be able to detect the emotions, plus as I've already mentioned there is the chance that someone is expressing outwardly a different set of emotions than what they really feel inside of them. This whole detection of emotions is a tricky affair and the AI cannot make conclusive conclusions about someone's emotional state. Instead, it would be used as an indicator and part of the "package" aspects of interpreting human communication such as spoken speech and gestures.

There are various levels of self-driving cars.

The topmost level is considered Level 5, and refers to an AI self-driving car that has the AI driving the car without any need for human intervention. In fact, often a Level 5 self-driving car will have no provision for human driving, doing so by having removed from the self-driving car any gas and brake pedals and removed the steering wheel.

For self-driving cars that are less than the Level 5, those such self-driving cars require a human driver be in the self-driving car and that the human driver be attentive and responsible at all times for the driving of the car. This means that even if the AI is co-sharing the driving task, the human driver is still on-the-hook. I mention this because I've mentioned many times abut the dangers of this co-sharing arrangement.

When a self-driving car is less than a Level 5, the question arises as to whether or not the human driver is actually paying attention to the roadway and the driving task. If the human driver becomes lulled into believing that the AI is doing just fine, it can create an untoward circumstance if the AI suddenly opts to hand the driving back to the human driver.

As such, there are various means to try and detect whether the human driver is staying active in the driving task. For example, the steering wheel might detect if their hands are present on the steering wheel, and there might be an inward facing camera that is detecting whether the driver's face is facing forward and whether their eyes are on-the-road.

Some believe that we should add the emotional state detection into the matter of trying to discern whether the human driver is paying attention to the driving task. This could be done via the visual, facial recognition of trying to detect emotions. It could be done by the audio detection of emotions by the nature of the words and sounds that the human driver might utter. And, we now know that it might also be possible via the breathing of the human driver, using RF signals to try and detect this.

The odds are high that most AI self-driving cars will have some form of WiFi included into them. This is likely done for the purposes of having human occupants that want to use WiFi, such as those traveling on a family trip and all have brought their laptops and smartphones with them. The WiFi might also be used for the OTA (Over The Air) updating of the AI self-driving car, which is a feature involving connecting the AI to a cloud capability to then share aspects up into the cloud and get updates pushed down into the self-driving car.

You might be saying to yourself that for a less than Level 5 self-driving car that it makes sense to be trying to gauge the emotion of the human driver, since it ties to the driving task, potentially, but why would a less than Level 5 self-driving car need to know the emotional state of the occupants?

Admittedly, knowing the emotional state of the occupants does not necessarily have as iron clad a rationale as does the case of the human driver. But, you could say that knowing the emotional state of the occupants could be quite handy. As mentioned earlier, the example of a human occupant that says to drive to the end of the pier might be interpreted differently if the AI is also examining the emotional status of the occupant.

There are other ways that the emotional state of the human occupants might come to play. Some good, some maybe bad, depending upon your viewpoint of the world. Let's assume that the advent of AI self-driving cars is likely to produce the ridesharing-as-a-service mania that most predict will happen. We're going to have ridesharing cars aplenty, with zillions of AI self-driving cars constantly roaming and at the ready to take us humans for a ride.

Inside a ridesharing AI self-driving car, there are likely to be ads, either pictures, video, streaming, or whatever. This will be a means to get some extra dough for the owner of the AI self-driving car, and perhaps a means to have a lessened cost to the human passenger for the ride. Similar to how I earlier provided the example of detecting an emotional reaction to a laundry soap ad, imagine how beneficial it might be to use the inward facing cameras of the AI self-driving car and perhaps the RF signal capabilities to determine the human occupant's emotional reaction to the in-car ads. Could be quite handy.

There are lots of other handy reasons to detect the human emotion involved. Maybe the AI could calm down a passenger that is overly distraught. Maybe the AI should contact someone such as emergency services if the person seems to be emotionally on the verge of some untoward act. And so on.

We must also ask though whether this is a violation of privacy. You might say that once you get inside the AI self-driving car, you've given up some amount of privacy by the act of getting into the AI self-driving car. We might also see regulation appear that will cover the privacy aspects of human occupants inside AI self-driving cars. Some point out that today when you get into a human driven ridesharing service you are already giving up various privacy aspects, and so they don't see this as any different than if the AI was driving. Anyway, it all needs to be sorted out.

In addition to detecting the emotions of humans inside an AI self-driving car, we might also consider the possibilities of detecting emotions of humans outside the AI self-driving car. A person steps up to the AI self-driving car and raises their hands in a threatening manner, as though they are going to pound on the hood of the self-driving car. Let's assume that the sensors of the AI self-driving car detect this person doing this, which is generally feasible to detect.

Should the AI self-driving car ignore the apparent actions of the person? Maybe this is a pedestrian aiming to do harm to the self-driving car and its occupants, if any. One might argue that if the AI could also detect the emotional state of the person, it might have a better chance of figuring out the intent of the person. We're though starting to veer again towards some challenging privacy issues. Suppose the AI self-driving car is driving down the street and meanwhile detecting the emotional state of every person that's walking, biking, sitting, crawling or in any means being seen by the AI system.

It is said that we humans have a sense of Emotional Intelligence (EI). Indeed, there are those that purport to be able to measure your degree of emotional capabilities via your Emotional Quotient (EQ) or your Emotional Intelligence Quotient (EIQ).

These measures are about our ability to detect the emotion in others, along with our own capability related to emotions.

With advances in computational capabilities and AI, we are getting closer to automated systems that can detect emotions and presumably react to them in an "intelligent" manner. AI self-driving cars will certainly benefit from this kind of capability, though we also need to recognize that it creates numerous ethical and privacy concerns too. I'd say that you should be ready for an emotional roller coaster ride on the way to figuring out how much emotional recognition we want in our AI self-driving cars.

CHAPTER 7

REAR-END COLLISIONS

AND

AI SELF-DRIVING CARS

CHAPTER 7

REAR-END COLLISIONS

AND

AI SELF-DRIVING CARS

Rear-end collisions. They can be a doozy. Let me share with you an example that happened to me some years ago.

I was stopped at a red light and idly looking around, awaiting a green light. My driver's side window was rolled down and it was a nice summer day with the sounds of birds chirping and I was on my way down to the beach for some R&R.

All of a sudden, in a seemingly split second, I heard a revving engine and I began to uncontrollably lurch forward and flop back-and-forth in the driver's seat – my car had been hit from behind by an accelerating car that had been approaching the red light (turns out, the senior citizen driver mistakenly hit the accelerator instead of the brake). He barreled into the rear of my car, shoving my car into the car ahead of me. The hit was so severe that it ruptured the gas tank of my car and petrol began to spill onto the ground. I was momentarily unconscious or somehow blacked out and nearby pedestrians rushed to help pull me out of my car. I lived to tell the tale.

As I mentioned, rear-end collisions can be a doozy. In this case, I was lucky that I was unhurt. My car had quite a bit of damage and it got repaired via my car insurance. The car ahead of me had damage. The car that hit me had damage. Miraculously, no one was actually injured in this rather scary cascading event. We were all lucky. It could have been a lot worse.

According to the National Highway Traffic Safety Administration (NHTSA), in the United States alone there are something like 6 million car accidents per year and about 40% of those involve rear-end collisions. The math there is that there are approximately 2.4 million rear-collisions each year. In that case, there's a rear-end collision in the United States on the average about every 13 seconds (approximately 31,536,000 seconds per year, divided by the approximate 2,400,000 rear-enders per year).

Statistics suggest that most of the rear-end collisions occur at speeds less than 10 miles per hour. Typical injuries to the occupants of the colliding cars includes whiplash, damage to the knees, spine twisting, sometimes brain concussions, etc. Fortunately, at lower speeds, rear-enders tend to not involve death, and instead it is mainly mild injuries and sometimes severe injuries. That being said, anyone that's harmed or crippled due to a rear-end collision has every right to be upset and angry that the situation arose.

How do rear-end collisions arise?

Let's consider that rear-end collisions involve a lead car and a follower car. The lead car is the one that's going to suffer being hit at the rear-end of the vehicle. The follower car is going to be the one that rams into the back of the lead car. That's the fundamental setup.

We can make this more complex by considering multiple rear-end collisions like my situation that had a car that was behind me (a follower) that hit my car (the lead car), and then I slid into the rear of the car ahead of me (in which case, I became a follower car and the car head of me became the lead car). Cascading rear-end collisions do happen and it's almost like a game of dominos, knocking down one domino causes it to hit the next, and the next, and so on. For the moment, allow me to concentrate on the fundamental use case of just two cars.

The two cars in a fundamental rear-end scenario can be in motion or at a standstill, just prior to the initiating of the rear-end collision event.

The senior citizen driving the car that was behind me, he was in motion and smacked into the rear of my car, of which my car was motionless at that point in time of the impact. My car then went into motion as a result of the impact and rammed into the motionless car ahead of me. This caused the car ahead of me to go into motion, but that car was at the front of the pack and fortunately after getting pushed forward there were no other nearby cars to get hit.

For the two cars involved in the foundational case, the motions can involve acceleration or deceleration. The senior citizen behind me had confused his accelerator pedal for the brake pedal, and he was trying to come to a full stop, so he was pushing down onto the pedal with great force. This meant he was pushing down forcibly on the accelerator pedal due to his confusion. That's also why I heard an engine revving noise just moments before the crash. It's also why the crash was strong enough to rupture my gas tank and push my car forward into the back of the car ahead of me.

In general, we then have the situation of a lead car and a follower car, of which they might be in motion, both or neither, and they might be accelerating or decelerating, just prior to the rear-end collision event.

This structure will help to explain a variety of rear-end collision circumstances.

Suppose a lead car is in motion and going at a speed of say 1 mile per hour (meaning that it is just barely crawling forward, and presumably not at a full-stop). Suppose that a follower car is going around 15 miles per hour and coming up upon the lead car. The follower car for whatever reason rams into the lead car, producing a rear-end collision. Both cars are merging into traffic onto an expressway.

This seems pretty much like an everyday kind of example of a rear-ender and on the surface there's nothing particularly noteworthy about it. Turns out this is a real example. Furthermore, it is noteworthy and newsworthy due to the aspect that the accident involved as the lead car was one of Apple's AI self-driving cars consisting of a specially outfitted Lexus SUV RX450h 2016.

Apple AI Self-Driving Car in a Rear-End Collision

Yes, in case you hadn't already heard about it, there was an incident of an Apple AI self-driving car that recently got involved into a rear-end collision, wherein it was hit from behind by a human-driven Nissan Leaf.

Both cars were merging from Rifer Road onto the Lawrence Expressway in Sunnyvale, California. This is a relatively popular roadway location that involves lots of car traffic. The incident occurred on Friday, August 24, 2018 at a reported 2:58 p.m. PDT. I'd guess that a late mid-afternoon incident on a Friday would not be out-of-the-ordinary per se, and there's often people rushing around on Friday afternoons in that location, wanting to get home from work and taking off a bit early, or maybe rushing back to the office after other off-site meetings, or maybe heading to a baseball game, etc.

Because Apple has registered for use of its AI self-driving cars onto California public roadways, it is also required to report accidents involving its cars, doing so via filing the Department of Motor Vehicles (DMV) form number OL316, entitled the "Report of Traffic Collision Involving an Autonomous Vehicle." The law requires that the report be filed within 10 business days of any such incident. In this case, the report was signed as Wednesday, August 29, 2018, thus about 5 days after the accident itself.

It was reported that both of the cars had some relatively minor damage. There were no reported injuries to humans. The weather at the time of the incident was clear, sunny, during daylight, and the road surface was dry. Both of the cars were proceeding straight. Thus, it was a textbook style rear-end collision.

At the Cybernetic AI Self-Driving Car Institute, we are developing AI software for self-driving cars, and we are earnestly interested in any incidents involving self-driving cars. There're always handy lessons to be learned, both for us and for the industry as a whole, and one might say for the public at large too.

When dealing with a mix of human driven cars and AI driven cars, there are four distinct combinations of the rear-end collision scenario – see Figure 1 on the next page.

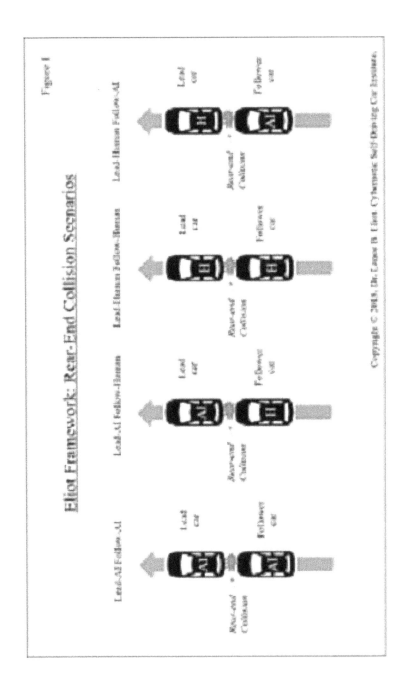

Just after the Apple Lexus incident was broadcast on the news, I had someone ask me an interesting question that perhaps illuminates the understanding and misunderstanding of the public's perception of AI self-driving cars.

I was asked this: "How could an AI self-driving car be involved in getting hit from behind in a rear-end collision, shouldn't it be smart enough to have avoided it?"

There's a lot to unpack in that question. It seemingly suggests that AI self-driving cars will be omnipresent and presumably never get into car accidents. I've in my writings and my speeches at industry conferences said repeatedly that we need to be careful of not over ascribing incredible super powers to AI self-driving cars. They are still cars, and they are still prone to the laws of physics.

Now, admittedly, it would be useful to know whether or not the Lexus was able to detect that the follower car was about to hit it. One would hope that the rear-facing sensors were able to discern that the Leaf was coming up at a fast pace and that there was a high likelihood that the Leaf was about to strike the Lexus.

For AI self-driving cars, per my framework, here's the key driving task aspects involved:

- Sensor data collection and interpretation
- Sensor fusion
- Virtual world model updating
- AI action planning
- Car controls command issuance

There are lots of questions that would fascinating to ask of Apple in this situation.

Did the Lexus detect the upcoming Leaf, plus, did the Lexus also try to identify a means of escape to avoid the incident or otherwise lessen the impact? The sensors hopefully detected the Leaf coming up behind the Lexus, and identified that it was a car coming up. The Lexus should have known it was doing the alleged 1 mile per hour and been able to detect the Leaf going at the reported 15 miles per hour. Simple math would have been able to ascertain that the pace of the Leaf was going to overtake the Lexus, based on the distances between them and the detectible speeds of both cars.

The virtual world model of the AI system for the Lexus should have been able to plot out the upcoming Leaf and made a prediction that the rear-end collision would likely occur. The AI action plan should have then tried to identify ways to avoid the incident, if feasible. For example, suppose the Lexus opted to rapidly accelerate, it might have had time to avoid getting hit from behind, or maybe lessened the impact by being at a closer matching speed of the Leaf.

It could be that accelerating was not a viable choice, given the distances and time available, and maybe the Lexus might have accelerated upon a car ahead and thus generated its own rear-end collision. So, another aspect might be to consider veering out of the path of the Leaf.

This though might not have been a good solution depending upon whether or not there was available room to the left or right to swerve and avoid being hit by the Leaf. Also, any such sudden maneuver could have other adverse consequences, possibly hitting something else such as a pole or other car, and since there were humans inside the Lexus it would preclude potentially doing such a radical maneuver that the maneuver itself might harm the human occupants – this is an ongoing ethical question about AI self-driving cars, as to having to have the AI make tough choices of this nature.

We don't yet know what was happening inside the AI of the Lexus.

Presumably, the AI development team of Apple has taken a close look to figure out what occurred. Maybe the AI did not live-up to the task at hand, so to speak, and needs more work on it to be able to deal with such incidents. Maybe the AI did everything it could have. If no other viable options seemed reasonable, it could be that the AI opted to just go ahead and take the rear-end collision. This could be a sound choice. Out of the myriad of options, sometimes the one that seems to involve no action might be the best, and the result in this case was apparently no human injuries, so in that sense the AI might have made a good choice. We don't know.

I've mentioned many times that just because we might not see any overt action by an AI self-driving car that it doesn't mean that it didn't nonetheless do all sorts of permutations on what to do. In the few seconds or split seconds leading up to a car crash, there might be a tremendous volley of computational analyses, all of which end-up at the "best" choice being to take no action. Thus, an outsider observing the self-driving car might be misled into believing that the AI did nothing at all. It's hard to say without cracking open the AI to ascertain what it did or did not do in the circumstance.

It's like a human driver that decided not to turn the wheel or hit the brakes, and afterward you might ask why, and the human might be able to tell you that they overtly made such a decision, or they might have not been aware of what was happening and thus took no action because they weren't able to think it through. As mentioned about my case of getting hit from behind by the senior citizen driver, I was blissfully unaware that the car was about to hit me (I was listening to chirping birds instead!). I did hear the revving of an engine, but it was a blur in my mind and the whole event unfolded so fast that I had no mental awareness of it occurring.

Now, you might counter-argue that I should have been looking in my rear-view mirror to see any cars coming up from behind me. I admit this is something I do from time-to-time, but not all of the time. How many of us are continually looking in our rear-view mirror while sitting at a red light and doing so because we think that a car behind us might ram into our car? I dare say few human drivers would do this. I did so for a few weeks after the incident, but gradually have let my guard down. But, that's a human for you.

The AI self-driving car has no such difficulty and should always be looking behind itself. Its sensors should always be on, and it should be undertaking continuously the cycle of sensor data collection and interpretation, sensor fusion, virtual world model updating, AI action planning, and issuing cars controls commands. Was the Lexus doing so? That's in the hands of the AI developers at Apple.

One of the weakest portions of most contemporary AI self-driving cars is their lack of looking behind them. Nearly all of the sensors and attention goes toward what's in front of the self-driving car. This certainly makes sense in terms of the rudiments of what an AI self-driving car needs to do. Some therefore consider looking behind the self-driving car as a kind of "edge" problem and less crucial. But, however you want to classify it, I think we would all agree that a well-rounded and properly proficient driving car should be doing some quite significant look-behinds.

Some have criticized the DMV regulations as being inadequate because it does not require the company that reports an incident to also explain what happened inside of the AI. There are those that believe it would be beneficial to all of us, the high-tech developers and the public and the regulators, if we knew why the AI might have faltered or not faltered in any given situation. The firms themselves suggest that this would not be helpful to anyone other than the firm itself, given the idiosyncratic aspects of each AI system and also that it could divulge proprietary secrets of the AI self-driving car involved.

I realize that some AI self-driving car pundits would say that there should never be any rear-end collisions involving AI self-driving cars, due to the belief that we should have only and exclusively AI self-driving cars on our roadways. In the case of the Apple Lexus, these pundits would point at the Leaf being driven by a human and exhort that it provides further proof that we need to get human drivers out of the equation, by getting those pesky human drivers off the roadways.

Please be aware that in the United States alone there are about 200+ million conventional cars. Those conventional cars are driven by humans. Those conventional cars are not going to suddenly become AI self-driving cars overnight. We are going to have a mix of human driven cars and AI self-driving cars, which will last for many years, likely decades.

In fact, some question whether we will ever get to a point of having only AI self-driving cars and there are some that cling to the belief that humans will still insist on being able to drive a car. This would become a regulatory issue of some likely contention, at least for the foreseeable future. Perhaps at some point down-the-road, we'll all be so used to AI self-driving cars that no one will want to actually humanly drive a car. Hard to foresee, but possible (or, maybe humans can drive cars on private roads and at car race tracks, but not on public roadways!).

Let's all agree that there are going to be situations of AI self-driving cars getting hit from behind by human driven cars, and that human driven cars are a reality for the foreseeable future. Sometimes, an AI self-driving car might be able to avoid such a collision, while sometimes not. Thus, it won't always happen, and it depends partially on the circumstances and whether the AI is good enough to be able to avoid a collision, if such avoidance is plausible.

Take a look at Figure 2 to see a matrix of the rear-end collision scenarios.

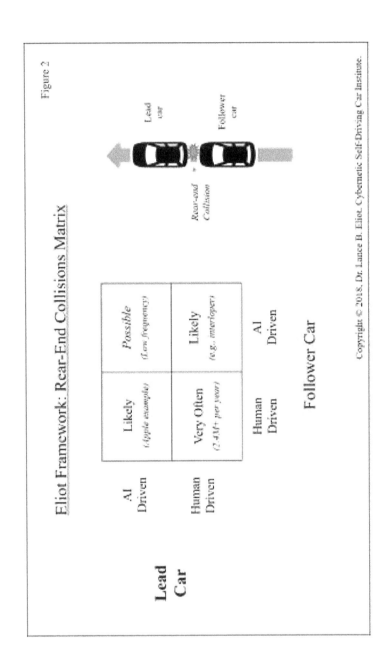

Figure 2

Will AI self-driving cars be the culprit that does a rear-end collision? Sure. I know that some pundits might say it won't ever happen, but again they fail to grasp the physics involved. Suppose a human driven car is ahead of the AI self-driving car. Thus, the human driven car is the lead car, and the AI self-driving car is the follower car. The lead car decides to slam on the brakes. What does the AI self-driving car do?

Assume that there's no place to swerve the AI self-driving car to avoid hitting the rear-end of the lead car. Let's go with a straight-ahead scenario. You might argue that the AI self-driving car should be able to detect the sudden deceleration of the lead car. I'd agree that it should be detectible by the AI self-driving car, and just to be on the safe side let's pretend that's a 99% time that it is detected (I'm going to leave 1% for situations wherein the sensors either fail or are otherwise unable to detect the car ahead – I realize that some will argue with me, in that some will say it should do so 100% of the time, while others might say it's more like 90% and 10%, and so on).

Okay, so we've got a suddenly decelerating lead car, and the AI self-driving car is the follow car. Can the AI self-driving car stop in time? You might contend that yes, it will always be able to do so, assuming that the AI is properly keeping a safe stopping distance away from the car ahead of it. Some believe that AI self-driving cars should always maintain the proper stopping distances. We know that humans do not do so, and that routinely we humans drive with too little stopping distance ahead of us.

Is it realistic to assume that an AI self-driving car will always be maintaining the proper stopping distance ahead of it? No. That's a completely unrealistic expectation. I'll give you a simple example as illustration.

While on a freeway, suppose an AI self-driving car has a proper stopping distance ahead of it, and meanwhile a car veers into the gap, cutting the distance between the AI self-driving car and the car now ahead of it.

The AI self-driving car would need to presumably slow down to try and arrive at a proper stopping distance from the interloper car. Even if the AI self-driving car is viably able to slow down in the given situation, for some moment in time there will be an improper stopping distance.

If the car that is the interloper suddenly jams on its brakes, the AI self-driving car is going to rear-end it, assuming that there's no other avoidable alternative. There's too little stopping distance for the AI self-driving car to come to a halt without hitting the interloper car.

Pundits would say that it's because the stupid human became the interloper. Stupid or not, the human driver is part of the equation and as I mentioned earlier they will be for many years to come. I suppose if we had a utopian world of all and only AI self-driving cars, the AI self-driving cars in theory could arrange themselves and communicate via say V2V (vehicle-to-vehicle) to avoid such situations. Not going to happen for a very long time.

Some pundits would also say it's unfair to "blame" the AI self-driving car in such a situation, since the human caused the incident. I'm not talking herein about the blame game, and only responding to the notion that somehow AI self-driving cars "cannot" ever rear-end another car. I believe that I've well-articulated now that it is quite easily possible for an AI self-driving car to ram into the rear of another car, regardless of who caused it to happen.

We've got these key situations:

- Rear-end scenario #01: Human driven follow car rams into a human driven lead car

- Rear-end scenario #02: AI driven follow car rams into a human driven lead car

- Rear-end scenario #03: Human driven follow car rams into an AI driven lead car

- Rear-end scenario #04: AI driven follow car rams into an AI driven lead car

For rear-end scenario #01, we already know that in the United States this happens around 2.4 million times a year (i.e., human driver rear-ends another human driven car).

For rear-end scenario #02, as discussed herein, we're going to have AI self-driving cars that will ram into human driven cars, either due to the human driver taking some untoward action, or perhaps due to something in the AI that presumably unintentionally goes awry.

For rear-end scenario #03, we've seen the Apple Lexus incident as an example of what's to come, namely that we're going to have human driven cars that ram into AI self-driving cars, of which hopefully the AI self-driving cars will try to avoid if at all feasible.

For rear-end scenario #04, pundits would say that there should never be an instance of an AI self-driving car that rams into another AI self-driving car.

In theory, the two AI self-driving cars should communicate and coordinate in such a manner that it would never occur. I don't think this is a very reasonable expectation. You cannot assume perfect communication, and nor can you assume that the AI self-driving cars will be operating perfectly. I say wake-up and smell the coffee, in the real-world this is going to happen and get ready for it.

As mentioned, there are rear-end collisions that are doozies and others that are not. The Apple Lexus incident was somewhat a fortunate occurrence in that it involved reportedly no human injuries, luckily so (of course, let's all hope for no such incidents). Had there been human injuries, I'm sure that the news media would have rocketed the story to the front-page headlines.

Sadly, such incidents involving AI self-driving cars are going to happen and we and the public need to be mentally prepared for it. The key will be to learn from the incidents and see what can be done to try and prevent them or mitigate the injuries and damages when they occur. Let's be safe other there.

CHAPTER 8

AUTONOMOUS NERVOUS SYSTEMS

AND

AI SELF-DRIVING CARS

CHAPTER 8

AUTONOMOUS NERVOUS SYSTEMS AND AI SELF-DRIVING CARS

The autonomic nervous system of humans is sometimes also referred to as the vegetative nervous system, or the visceral nervous system, or even the sympathetic nervous system. We all know that whatever you call it, the purpose seems to be as a regulatory function of the human body and one that generally occurs automatically. In that sense, it happens seemingly unconsciously.

Your brain doesn't apparently need to do much toward making sure that your heart is pumping blood. Cardiac regulation is mainly the role of the autonomic nervous system. Respiratory functioning is also usually being handled by the autonomic nervous system. Overall, the autonomic nervous system (ANS) is often considered the true core of our fight-or-flight response mechanism. It offers the handling of our key physiological responses. Most of the time it is happening in an involuntary fashion. It just happens and we live to tell the tale.

The other day, while studying some AI code that had been jointly written in Python and TensorFlow with a colleague of mine, he sneezed. This wouldn't be particularly noteworthy except for the fact that he sneezed again, and again, and again. He somehow got himself into a sneezing fit. Was he allergic to Python? Maybe to TensorFlow?

Maybe to AI? All kidding aside, it was quite a moment that caught both him and I unawares and he seemed to just keep sneezing. The first sneezes were almost humorous, but when he kept going it became more somber and we both wondered if somehow there was something amiss. Fortunately, it subsided, disappearing almost as mysteriously as it had originally appeared.

It might have been that his autonomic nervous system was reacting to an environmental condition, perhaps some allergen in the air or maybe the coffee he was drinking had some chemical that sparked the sneezing. Thus, one theory would be that it was entirely due to an involuntary act and a foundational human response that he had no conscious role in instituting and nor controlling.

Or, it could be that he was mentally reacting to our conversation and perhaps his mind was jogging his sneezing mechanism as a type of reaction or communication mechanism. In the old debate of mind over matter, we'll likely never know whether it was a straightforward autonomic response or whether it was possibly a mentally generated response.

Some liken the autonomic nervous system to being a "second brain" of the human body. It's as though we have our normal brain that we believe does our thinking for us, and then a second kind-of-brain that is the "body controller" aka the autonomic nervous system and for which it tends to do whatever it wants to do. At times, the two brains (if you believe in this notion) are aligned and at other times they might be working seemingly separately. Your real mind might be saying don't sneeze, and the second "mind" might be saying sneeze and sneeze some more. The real mind might not be able to do much to stop the second mind.

Now, one could suppose that the real mind could try to trick or control the second mind, in some cases and in some ways. While my colleague was sneezing, he grabbed for a glass of water and tried to drink the water. He later explained to me that he thought perhaps he could suppress or even stop the sneezing by guzzling down some water. Turns out this didn't seem to make any difference to the matter and he kept sneezing. But, it is perhaps illustrative that his real brain had mentally come up with a quick plan of drinking water, doing so in hopes of overcoming the "second brain" of the sneezing fit being fueled by presumably his autonomic nervous system.

We might consider Robert Louis Stevenson's famous Dr. Jekyll and Mr. Hyde as the same kind of duality of having two brains in our body. The real brain provides our presumably conscious kinds of thinking, while the "second brain" of the autonomic nervous system deals with our visceral, vegetative kinds of responses. Of course, Henry Jekyll was meant to represent good and Edward Hyde was representing evil, which in the case of the human body and its "two brains" as alluded to herein we aren't saying one is good versus the other being evil. They both just are.

They each perform their respective function. At times they might be well aligned, and at other times they might be misaligned, including perhaps wanting the opposite of each other. For whatever reason, the autonomic nervous system might be saying sneeze, darn you, sneeze, while the real brain is saying let's put an end to this disruptive and seemingly useless and unfitting sneezing fit.

What does this have to do with AI self-driving cars?

At the Cybernetic AI Self-Driving Car Institute we are developing AI systems for self-driving cars. One of the crucial open questions right now involves the role of so-called autonomic subsystems versus AI-led subsystems of an AI self-driving car.

Allow me to elaborate.

Many conventional cars today have an automatic braking system that is included by the car manufacturer. Often it is an added optional feature for your car. If you opt to pay for it, the feature is added to or included into your car. Don't confuse this with the anti-lock braking system (ABS), which has been around for many years and comes pretty much as standard on most cars today. Instead, I'm referring to what is often called the Advanced Emergency Braking (AEB) system or at times referred to as the Automatic Emergency Braking or the

Autonomous Emergency Braking. Either way you phrase it, let's anoint it as the AEB herein.

The National Highway Traffic Safety Administration (NHTSA) pushed for the full adoption of AEB in the United States and by-and-large the auto makers agreed to do so by the year 2022. The notion is that it is an autonomic subsystem of your car, meaning that it acts independently of the human driver and tries to figure out when to apply the brakes, doing so only when it is considered an "emergency" situation and also doing so in the somewhat blind hope that applying the brakes is the right thing to do in the circumstance.

Notice that the way in which I've phrased the nature of the AEB is by carefully pointing out that it is intended to do more good than harm, though you need to keep in mind that it is a relatively simplistic subfunction and might be right or wrong when it opts to engage. If it detects an object in front of your car, and if your car seemingly is going to hit that object, the AEB deduces mathematically that it should go ahead and apply the brakes on your behalf as the human driver.

You generally don't have much say about this. The AEB generally does its detection and calculations in split seconds and then activates the brakes. You might liken this to the human autonomic nervous system and consider it to be a reflexive or autonomic act of the car. In terms of the example earlier about sneezing, the autonomic nervous system of my colleague presumably invoked his sneezing fit, and his real brain didn't have much to do with it. In the case of the AEB, you the human driver and with your real brain, generally don't have much sway over the activation of the AEB and the AEB will do what it needs to do.

In some cars, you as the human driver can choose to disengage or deactivate the AEB. This raises all sorts of questions though. Why would you deactivate the AEB? In theory, if your car has AEB in it, you would want it to always be on, always be ready, always be available to automatically apply the brakes in an effort to save your life and possibly the lives of others. Some auto makers are prohibiting the car owner or consumer from being able to turn-off the AEB. It is considered essential and not to be toyed with. But, there are some car owners or consumers that believe they should be able to decide for themselves whether or not to have the AEB activated. Freedom of choice is their mantra.

Suppose a conventional car that is equipped with AEB comes upon another car that is stopped in the roadway and the AEB detects the stopped object and applies the brakes to your car and manages to stop prior to hitting the other car. The AEB is the hero! The human driver for whatever reason wasn't noticing the stopped car or froze-up and failed to hit the brakes, and so the AEB stepped in like superman and applied the brakes.

Imagine if the AEB had not been engaged. As far as we can discern, the moving car would have plowed into the stopped car, possibly causing injury or death. If you were in the car that got rear-ended, you'd want to know why the AEB had been disengaged on the car that hit you. It would seem irresponsible that the driver had deactivated the AEB, a mechanism that could have possibly saved lives and prevented injuries. This kind of circumstances is exactly why some of the auto makers make the AEB unable to be deactivated by the consumer (often, it can instead be deactivated by a trained car mechanic or by the auto maker).

Besides the ability to possibly disengage beforehand the AEB, there is also often a feature of the AEB that allows for a type of "human action" default override of the AEB. For example, some AEB subsystems will detect whether the driver of the car is accelerating, and if so the AEB will not apply the brakes, even if the AEB has calculated that there seems to be an emergency and that applying the brakes seems like the better choice. This capability of the AEB is made under the assumption that if the human driver is accelerating, perhaps the human has determined that the best course of action involves speeding up to avoid a crash. In that case, the AEB quietly demurs to the choice of the human driver.

This brings up the duality of the two brains. You have a human driver that has all the intelligence of a human and therefore we might assume that for driving of the car they know best. We have a "dumb" advanced emergency braking system that relies upon very simplistic mathematical formulas and sensors of the car to try and figure out whether to apply the brakes in what appears to be emergency situations.

Should the AEB always go ahead and apply the brakes when it ascertains what it believes to be an emergency situation, or should we allow that a human might be more aware of what's really happening and therefore in some situations defer to the human?

That's the million dollar question. Under what circumstance should the AEB apply? You might say that the AEB should just ask the human driver, hey, you, should I go ahead and apply the brakes right now. But, that's not very practical. By definition, the AEB is generally going to undertake braking at the last moment, when just split seconds are left, and the time it would require to ask a human whether to go ahead and apply the brakes would defeat the purpose of the AEB. By the time it asked and the human responded, the odds are that the car would have already smashed into whatever the AEB was trying to prevent a crash from occurring.

We're kind of back to the predicament about whether to allow a human to deactivate the AEB. Some say that the AEB should be sacrosanct. It should always be on. It should always proceed to apply the brakes when it ascertains that applying the brakes is warranted. Period. No further discussion or debate. There are those that point out that the AEB is a simplistic function and might or might not be right in what it chooses to do. For them, the AEB should either be allowed to be deactivated by a human, beforehand, prior to an emergency, or that during an emergency the acts of the human driver should determine whether or not the AEB acts, such as if the human driver is accelerating deeply then it implies the human is overtly trying to act and the AEB should not mess with the human driver.

Indeed, this brings up another salient point. Suppose the human driver was rapidly accelerating and genuinely believed that by accelerating they might get themselves out of a jam and avoid crashing. Meanwhile, suppose the AEB was blind to whatever the human driver was doing and figured that it made no difference whatsoever about the acts of the human driver. As such, all of a sudden, the AEB applies the brakes. The human driver is confused and confounded since they are trying to do the direct opposite. If both the AEB and the human driver are at odds, one can assume that the end result will be worse, namely that the car won't necessarily brake in time and nor will the car accelerate in time to avoid the incident. Boom. Crash.

The same issue can confront AI self-driving cars.

I know it might seem surprising to consider that the same predicament can face AI self-driving cars. You would likely be under the impression that the AI of a self-driving car would determine all the actions of the self-driving car. But, this is not necessarily the case.

Many of the auto makers and tech firms are taking "conventional cars" and adding the AI self-driving car capabilities into those cars. Thus, it is not a grassroots from the bottom-up redesign of a car, but instead the morphing of a somewhat conventional car into an AI self-driving car. As such, there are a wide variety of elements of a conventional car that are still embodied in the arising AI self-driving car.

In essence, once again we have two brains in a car. For a conventional car, it's the human driver and the AEB. For a true AI self-driving car, it is the AI and the AEB. Well, actually, there are other semi-autonomous subfunctions of a conventional car that also relate to this whole notion of who's in-charge of the driving, but the AEB is the most prominent and the focus herein. You can apply the same principles underlying the AEB matter to the other kinds of autonomous rudimentary functions on conventional cars.

Just as the human driver is the "real brain" and the AEB is the (shall we say) tiny brain, in the same manner we might ascribe that the AI of the self-driving car is the "real brain" and the AEB is the tiny brain. I want to be careful though in somehow implying or suggesting that the AI is the equivalent to a human brain of a human driver – it is not. Therefore, when I refer to the word "brain" as it relates to the AI, I am only using the word in a loose sense and not intending to suggest it is equivalent.

For an AI self-driving car, you've got the dilemma of having the AI that is supposed to be doing the driving, and yet also there's an autonomic nervous system that consists of the AEB (and other subsystems). Which of them is in-charge?

You might contend that the AI should be in-charge. As such, you would presumably deactivate the AEB beforehand, prior to the AI driving the self-driving car. Thus, there's no need for the AI to be concerned about the AEB and avert any efforts by the AEB that might seem counter to whatever the AI is trying to do while driving the car. Matter settled.

But, not so fast! We are still going to be faced with the same concerns as we did with the human driver that deactivates beforehand the AEB. Suppose there is a situation in which the AI was faced with a situation that could have been solved via the use of AEB, but because the AEB was deactivated the AI instead took some action that then led into the crash.

If this seems theoretical, allow me to point out that this very same question arose with the Uber crash in Arizona that killed a pedestrian crossing the street. The Uber self-driving car had the AEB deactivated. The AI that was driving the Uber self-driving car hit a pedestrian. If the AEB had been activated, the question remains whether or not the Uber self-driving car would have struck the pedestrian, or that if it had done so nonetheless that at least it might have been going at a slower speed due to the braking of the AEB by the time it hit the pedestrian.

We've got the issue of whether to deactivate the AEB beforehand, and also the other question about what to do if the AEB is activated and it tries to override the AI of the self-driving car. Uber formally came out after the Arizona crash and pointed out that they had purposely deactivated the AEB since they believe that the self-driving car would otherwise possibly exhibit erratic driving behavior. This explanation fits with the points herein about the difficulties of driving a car when there are "two brains" involved and not necessarily working fully aligned.

At industry conferences, when I give presentations about AI self-driving cars, I often get asked the question of why t the AI of the self-driving car couldn't do the same thing that the AEB was doing. We all get the idea that the AEB is different from a human in that it is a piece of automation and it can takeover for a human by applying the brakes in a sudden and deep manner. But, since it is a piece of automation, and since the AI is a piece of automation, it seems odd and maybe troubling to not have them fully aligned with each other. They should presumably be one and the same.

As mentioned earlier, the AEB is typically on a conventional car and when an AI self-driving car capability is grafted onto a conventional car you then end-up with these kinds of disparities. It's almost like a Frankenstein containing multiple body parts from different sources. It's not easy to make sure they are all integrated together.

You might rightfully wonder why the AI of the self-driving car doesn't subsume the AEB function and perform the same tasks as the AEB would. In theory, we don't need an AEB per se if the AI embodies the same capabilities of an AEB. That's a good point.

The AI of most self-driving cars of today is not as well optimized to perform in the same manner as an AEB.

You can liken this to humans, in the duality of our minds and the autonomic nervous system. The autonomic nervous system works very fast and offers speed as an advantage for handling certain circumstances. When you put your hand near a hot stove, your hand recoils nearly instantly at the sensation of the heat. Some would say that this is happening in an autonomic fashion. Rather than your hand relaying to the brain that there is something hot, and your brain then figuring out what to do, including possibly sending a signal to the hand telling it to move away from the heat, the autonomic nervous system just makes it so.

One possibility in the Uber incident was that the AI might have taken too long to try and ascertain what action to take. If instead the AEB had been activated, it's conceivable that the AEB would have acted like the retrieval of a hand that's dangling over a hot stove, namely the AEB would have slammed on the brakes, right or wrong, in an autonomic manner.

In this particular case, we can likely surmise that the AEB would have been doing the right thing, based on what is known to-date about the circumstance. But, remember that the AEB would have presumably been activated all of the time, if it were activated at the time of the incident, and so you'd have had other tussles between the AEB and the AI, which might have led to other incidents. We don't know.

And so this takes us to the gamble that most of the auto makers and tech firms are right now taking. Should they leave the AEB activated on their emerging AI self-driving cars, or should they deactivate it. If they deactivate it, there is the later question to be asked when an incident occurs as to whether or not they were right to have deactivated the AEB. If they don't deactivate the AEB, it could turn out that there are situations where the AI and the AEB fight each other and the result is an incident that might otherwise have been avoided.

Darned if you do, darned if you don't.

That being said, there are AI developers that also say that we need to better integrate the AI and the AEB. We need to design the AI to take into account the AEB. This might also mean that the AEB should be redesigned, doing so in light of the advent of AI self-driving cars. The notion is that the AI and the AEB are woven together, integrated as it were, rather than two different capabilities that happen to be on the same self-driving car. That makes sense and it's the path we're pursuing.

You might have seen in 2015 a viral video that showed a Volvo that was being demonstrated as to its AEB capability. The short clip of just thirty seconds or so became a worldwide sensation because it showed a Volvo being driven forward and a human stood in front of the car, anticipating that the AEB would hit the brakes prior to the Volvo hitting the human. Instead, the Volvo hits the human. Some wisecracks posted with the video included that the feature should be renamed the Auto Leg Breaker, or that it is the safest car in the world but only if you are sitting inside of the car.

It turns out that after the video rose to attention, it was discovered that the particular Volvo shown in the video did not have the AEB pedestrian feature in it. People that were criticizing Volvo, did so falsely, and assumed that the feature was in the car and that the feature was engaged. That's part of the fake news in the AI self-driving car realm and something I've warned about many times.

The point to that story is that when you get into a car, you often don't really know what it consists of. Likewise, when standing outside of a car, you don't know for sure what's under-the-hood. Right now, we have a brewing and bubbling issue of the AI versus the AEB in terms of AI self-driving cars. I can predict that we'll have another incident involving an AI self-driving car that also had AEB, and for which the question of whether using the AEB would have been a life saver will arise. We've got to get the autonomic nervous system and the AI to be better integrated, soon. And that's nothing to sneeze at, I assure you.

CHAPTER 9
HEIGHT WARNINGS
AND
AI SELF-DRIVING CARS

CHAPTER 9

HEIGHT WARNINGS

AND

AI SELF-DRIVING CARS

Watch out for that low hanging bridge! If you live in Boston, you are likely familiar with the notion of getting "storrowed" (there's even a hastag for it). On Storrow Drive, there are numerous warning signs and blinking lights that forewarn you about a bridge that has only about an 11-foot clearance, and yet somehow drivers ram into it anyway.

This can be somewhat explained as to the confusion about ramming it due to the aspect that when new students show-up for college in Boston, they often rent a vehicle that either is higher than 11 feet or pile stuff on top of vehicles that ends-up being higher than 11 feet. They then use Storrow Drive to get to their university and sadly, regrettably, either ignore, disbelieve, or plain out don't see the warning signs about the low bridge height. As old saying goes, when a movable object strikes an unmovable one, the moving object is going to lose out.

Though the Bostonian bridge story has some attention, perhaps the grand winner for low bridges and incidents goes to the 11 foot 8 inch bridge nicknamed The Can-Opener. It's a railroad bridge located in Durham, North Carolina and more formally known as the Norfolk Southern–Gregson Street Overpass. Believe it or not, there is a crash into the bridge at least once per month. That's a high frequency.

You might be thinking that someone ought to do something about this situation, such as raising the bridge (expensive since it would involve dealing with the railroad tracks too) or possibly lowering the street (expensive since there are major sewer lines at a shallow depth). In lieu of being able to adjust the height, they've put up numerous warning signs. Nonetheless, trucks and especially rental trucks seem to have a magnetic attraction to trying to smash into The Can-Opener.

Interestingly, there doesn't seem to be a federal mandated height maximum requirement for commercial vehicles, and the states are able to set their own height maximum restrictions. Typically, the maximum height allowed for a commercial vehicle is around 13 ½ feet to 14 feet or so. Any bridge that such a vehicle wants to pass under must therefore be at least 14 feet or more in height. Preferably, there should be a few inches to spare.

Most passenger cars are around 5 to 6 feet in height. This leaves usually plenty of room to spare for getting under most bridges and overpasses. There are some SUV's though that push over the 6 foot size and include the rather tallish Hummer H2 which is 79 inches in height. Fortunately, most of these even higher passenger types of vehicles will still by-and-large be low enough to make it under any reasonable positioned bridge or overpass.

A good friend of mine used to work for Sears when he was in college and his job involved helping people tie things down to the tops of their cars. He tells wild stories of people that bought rather large pieces of furniture and insisted that it had to be tied down to the top of their cars so they could haul it home. Though he never had anyone come back and say that the height got them in trouble, he tells me that there were circumstances that likely would have had potential troubles if they had encountered The Can-Opener.

I remember one time I was traveling in someone's SUV and they drove into an underground parking structure. The designers of the parking structure must have not been very savvy since there were all sorts of pipes and plumbing hanging from the already low ceiling. The person driving the SUV had a ski rack on top of the SUV, and he was quite sure that it would clear the distance. As he squeezed into a parking spot, we heard a loud and foreboding scarping sound. Sure enough, we got out of the SUV and could see that he had wedged the ski rack up to one of the low hanging pipes.

I suppose that if you are going to indeed hit an immovable object like the underside of a bridge, you'd at least be somewhat better off if the thing that hits is something added to the top of your vehicle. Smashing up that dining room chair that's tied to the roof of your car is likely better than smashing the actual roof of your vehicle. If you watch some of the YouTube videos of trucks ramming into the lower parts of a bridge or overpass, the instances that involve the whole truck structure hitting and nearly exploding from the impact are the most excruciating to watch and lead to the most damage. Presumably, for a typical passenger car, and any such top oriented close-call shavings will be as a result of something piled on top of the car, and not hopefully take off the entire roof of the car.

For those of you that always carefully look for the roadway warning signs about heights, I applaud you, but I'd bet that most people don't pay attention to those signs. If you are driving a typical passenger car, you likely never look at the height warning signs and consider them as nothing more than a billboard that can be ignored. When you rent a truck or put stuff onto the top of your car, presumably you should have the presence of mind to suddenly become aware of height. Not everyone though thinks that way. As a result, they fall into the rut of always ignoring the warning signs about heights and get themselves into some tight pickles.

You could also nearly excuse some of the instances by the aspect that there are warning signs about heights that are at times themselves hard to spot. Perhaps at one point earlier on, the warning sign was highly visible, but after a while there are trees that grow near them or other roadway obstacles that can obscure those height warnings. I've seen graffiti on those signs. I've seen other roadway signs placed near to the height warning sign and it becomes a visually cluttered indication of the many things that you are supposed to be forewarned about.

In essence, it can sometimes be tricky to be able to readily see and read a height warning sign, even when you are purposely and intently trying to do so. Of course, situations like the Boston and the Durham examples are exceptions since they've gone out of their way to make sure there are plenty of such signs. Those signs even include blinking lights. Probably the next step would be a bullhorn that blares out something like "low bridge ahead, watch out!" I'm sure that those young students heading to college as a freshman would welcome such a warning (versus imagine the mess they must deal with before even starting class in terms of trying to deal with having rammed into a bridge with a rental truck!).

If you are lucky enough to spot a height warning sign and can make sense of it, presumably you would use the added awareness to judge whether your car can fit under the height stated. I'd bet there are some instances of human drivers that aren't exactly sure whether they'll be able to get their vehicle to fit under the height and rather than being cautious they take a chance anyway. Some of those chances likely turn out to be a bad bet and they end-up hitting the obstruction.

Supposing though that you do realize that you are cutting it close or that you won't fit, and so you opt to avoid going under the bridge or overpass. This can itself present another problem, since you need to figure out an alternative path to get to wherever you are going. Plus, you need to figure out soon enough before you reach the bridge or overpass such that you can legally and without being unsafe be able to make a driving maneuver to avoid the obstruction. In some of the online videos it seems apparent that the driver realized at the last moment what was going to happen and was unable to avoid hitting the bridge or overpass because they were already going too fast to stop in time or be able to undertake a maneuver to avoid the hit.

What does this have to do with AI self-driving cars?

At the Cybernetic AI Self-Driving Car Institute, we are developing AI systems for self-driving cars. One of the so-called "edge" problems involves having the AI be able to deal with height restrictions and circumstances such as avoiding striking a low hanging bridge or overpass.

I mentioned that this is an edge problem. Allow me to explain. An edge problem is considered a type of problem that is not considered at the core of an overall problem and instead is at the periphery. It is something that is identified as a problem but given less priority and attention than the core ones. In the case of an AI self-driving car, focusing on the general driving task is at the core, while providing attention to something like the height aspects is considered an edge because it is less likely to occur and somewhat of a rarity for a car.

That being said, it is something that those developing AI for self-driving trucks must consider at the core due to the higher likelihood of a truck encountering a height related issue. Thus, whether developed for the purposes of a car or truck, it is a feature that has value and needs to ultimately be considered "solved" in that the AI must have a means to contend with height related considerations.

There is another circumstance involving AI self-driving cars wherein height comes to play. If an AI self-driving car is towing something, such as a U-Haul rented storage carrier, the towed item might involve height related considerations. Though the self-driving car itself might not have any particular height related difficulties, the items being towed might be high enough to raise up to a low hanging bridge or overpass. Since the towed item is connected to the self-driving car, it's up to the AI to presumably be aware of what it is towing and therefore take into account changes needed in the driving task due to the towed item.

It's not an excuse to pretend that the AI was only responsible for the self-driving car per se. For a true level 5 self-driving car, which is considered the topmost ranking of an AI self-driving car, the assumption is that the AI can drive the car as a human would. In that sense, it would normally be an expectation that a human driving a car that's towing something is as responsible for the actions of the car as they are of the items towed. If the human fails to properly tie down the towed items or fails to connect them securely to the car, it's all on the human for having not done so. Likewise, if the human hits a bridge with the towed item, it's the driver's fault, whether a human driver or the AI.

As an overall framework of the AI driving tasks, here's the major steps that the AI undergoes while at the wheel of a self-driving car (so to speak):

- Sensor data collection and interpretation
- Sensor fusion
- Virtual world model updating
- AI action planning
- Car controls command issuance

Let's start with the aspect of the AI needing to know the height of the self-driving car, which would encompass the self-driving car plus anything piled on top of it, plus anything being towed by the self-driving car.

There's no easy automatic way right now for the AI to become aware of the height aspects. There aren't usually sensors on an AI self-driving car that will allow it to determine its own height and nor the height of something being towed. In the future, there might be such sensors added onto AI self-driving cars. For the moment, this being an edge problem doesn't tend to warrant the cost and effort of including such sensors onto an AI self-driving car.

If there isn't any such sensor already built-in, how else can the AI self-driving car ascertain the height of itself and whatever it might be towing? One means would be to ask about the height. The AI could ask a human. If there is a human that will either be occupying the AI self-driving car during the journey, or a human that is setting the AI along on a journey (but not going to riding in the self-driving car), the AI could ask about the height aspects.

You might assume that the human(s) involved would be wise enough to forewarn the AI about any height related considerations. I'd dare say that the human(s) might assume that the AI is already somehow able to figure out the height related aspects, and so the human(s) involved might be later shocked when they find out that their clothes and furniture spilled onto the highway because the towed storage shed bashed into the ceiling of a bridge. Probably would be best to have the AI inquire prior to a journey.

Even if the AI asks about the height, it doesn't imply necessarily that the human(s) will accurately reply. In that manner, the AI is either going to be stuck with assuming that the human indication is correct or might need to assume that the human is maybe off-base a bit and become extra cautious. If a human says that the height is around 9 feet, it might be prudent for the AI to assume that it is really more like 10 feet and therefore avoid any height circumstances involving 10 feet rather than only those at 9 feet.

Indeed, you might opt to default that if the human indicates there is any added height at all, the rule-of-thumb for the AI might be to avoid any kind of height restricted situations, though this is a rather extreme precaution and would likely cause the driving path of the self-driving car to become quite convoluted.

Another approach to potentially figuring out the height of an AI self-driving car would be for the AI to try and communicate with other AI self-driving cars around it. Another AI self-driving car might be able to discern the height related aspects, doing so by using its sensors such as its cameras, radar, sonic, and LIDAR. This could then be relayed to the self-driving car via V2V (vehicle-to-vehicle) communications. Thus, one AI self-driving car asks another nearby one to take a look, which after inspecting the height then is reported back to the asking AI self-driving car. Kind of a buddy system.

This brings up another facet of the height related problem. At some point, once there are lots of AI self-driving cars on the roadways, it could be that via the use of V2V that the AI systems are trying to help each other out. While on a freeway, if there's a car stalled in the middle of the freeway, those AI self-driving cars nearest to the stalled car can convey to other self-driving cars that are coming up upon the scene to be wary of the stalled car. In a similar manner, AI self-driving cars that are coming upon a low hanging bridge or overpass can potentially forewarn other approaching AI self-driving cars about the situation.

In the case of the Storrowed in Boston, there would be AI self-driving cars that might not yet know about the low overhang and meanwhile others that do (having driven that way before). The ones that knew about it, either due to having driven there before or upon detecting it or having been previously informed about it, could warn other AI self-driving cars that are nearby and that are headed toward the potential obstruction. The AI of the receiving self-driving cars would then need to ascertain whether the awareness about the low hanging circumstance applied to them or not.

We are also heading toward V2I, which is vehicle-to-infrastructure communication. There will be Internet of Things (IoT) types of devices along and throughout the roadway infrastructure and they will serve to warn drivers about various roadway conditions. These warnings might include that there's road construction up ahead, or maybe that an intersection is blocked and to avoid it, and so on. It is anticipated that road signs are likely to be augmented with IoT, thus rather than having to only be able to visually spot a road sign, the road sign will transmit an electronic signal and thus cars can be aware of what the road sign depicts (including speed limits, cautions, and of course height warnings).

Another consideration about AI self-driving cars is that they are likely to be on our roadways quite a bit. It is anticipated that many of the AI self-driving cars will be operating nearly non-stop, running 24x7. This is due to the belief that doing so makes economic sense and why not leverage the ability to have an electronic driver that never sleeps. From a height perspective, it implies that with these AI self-driving cars continually roving around there's perhaps a heightened chance (pun!) of them encountering height related driving circumstances. Thus, again another reason to have the AI prepared for such a situation.

You might be saying to yourself that the GPS and electronic maps ought to be letting the AI know about any height restrictions on the roadways. Currently, GPS mappings are somewhat inconsistent in having marked or indicated the height related aspects of a driving situation. It definitely is another source of input about heights and the AI should be considering it. Nonetheless, it is not always guaranteed to be available and the AI needs to be finding alternative ways to further figure out the height of obstructions.

The other day, I was driving through a rather tony neighborhood that had large trees at the sides of the streets and the trees had grown over the street to make a spectacular kind of shroud. It was breathtaking. But, there had been recent rains and high-winds, which caused some of the heavy branches to slightly break and bend downward. Driving along the street required some pretty careful weaving from one side of the street to the other, hoping to avoid hitting the dangling branches.

A true AI self-driving car should have been able to be equally deft in maneuvering through those streets. There would not have been any GPS mapping warnings. There weren't any street signs warning about the height issues. It was instead entirely in-the-moment of trying to figure out the height issues. Notice also that I drove "illegally" by going onto the other side of the street, momentarily, cautiously, only when safe to do so. I mention this point about driving "illegally" because there are some AI pundits that have claimed that AI self-driving cars should never drive illegally, which I've debunked as an unreasonable expectation.

In recap, the AI needs to discover the height of the self-driving car and which would include any towed items. It needs to be aware of height related restrictions, doing so via using its own sensors to try and identify height related concerns, along with trying to spot and read height warning signs, and possibly use GPS mappings, V2V, and V2I too. The AI should route around any height concerns, if feasible. If the AI is taken by surprise and comes upon a height problem, it needs to devise rapidly an action plan to safely maneuver to avoid the crash. If somehow a crash nonetheless occurs, the AI would need to become aware that a hit has occurred and take further action as appropriate.

As humans, we take for granted our ability to deal with height related driving issues. It is just the daily aspects of driving a car. Most of the time, we don't encounter height related problems. But, we are overall generally ready for it.

Some humans regrettably aren't paying attention or at times ignore or disbelieve when they get themselves into a height driving predicament. For AI systems that control self-driving cars, we're all going to want and expect that the AI is on the alert and able to contend with height aspects. As you can perhaps discern, it's a bit of a "tall order" for the AI to do so (aha, another pun!).

CHAPTER 10
FUTURE JOBS
AND
AI SELF-DRIVING CARS

CHAPTER 10

FUTURE JOBS
AND
AI SELF-DRIVING CARS

Jobs. Can't live without them, yet have to live by them. A Gallup poll indicated that 85% of employees hate their jobs. Yikes, that's a lot! Or, I suppose, you might wonder what those other 15% do that makes then not hate their jobs, and whether maybe they are either blind to hating their job or stubbornly won't fess up to it.

There are jobs of the past that no longer make sense and you'd be hard pressed to find someone that still performs the job. Included in these past jobs are being a switchboard operator, an ice block cutter, a knocker-upper (someone that was a human alarm clock and was paid to wake-up factory workers to come to work on-time), a lamplighter, a log driver, and so on.

To illustrate how jobs can become popular and then shrink in size, consider the plight of the switchboard operator. At one point in time, there were an estimated 100,000 switchboard operators in the United States. For those of you too young to remember this position, it involved connecting people that were trying to call each other on the phone. Today's automation takes care of this task and the switchboard operator became extinct.

Being aware of which jobs are "in" and which jobs are "out" can be important for a variety of reasons. The economy can be impacted when jobs disappear, and likewise be impacted when new jobs appear. Society also is impacted by having people decide what kinds of jobs they might be able to get and what the requirements are for those jobs. If you are in a job classification that's on its way out, you would be wise to try and retool for a job that's already in or might soon be coming in.

For those of you with children, I know it might seem hard to already be thinking about what they'll do for work in the future, but sadly it is something that you need to confront. If your child is already in high school, it implies they are either coming into the workforce in maybe four years or less, or if they are going to go to college then you need to consider what they'll be doing in about eight years from now. Steering your child toward a job as a switchboard operator would obviously not be prudent. I say that in jest, but also with some seriousness in that you'd want to identify whether a seemingly existing occupation will really be in existence at least four to eight years from now (there were some that were still getting trained to be switchboard operators, right up to and during the time that those jobs faded out)

Predicting future jobs is somewhat chancy. There are jobs that might appear or might not. There are jobs that might appear but perhaps at a later date than you predicted. There are jobs that will appear and require a very specific set of skills and capabilities. There are jobs that will grow and be plentiful, and other new jobs that will be very narrow, and few will be able to get those jobs. Jobs, jobs, jobs.

So, anyway, suppose we look ahead to the 2020's and the 2030's and try to predict what kinds of jobs might appear. The ones in the 2020's isn't that far away in time, and so we're then trying to use a crystal ball to see maybe five to 10 years from now. The ones in the 2030's is a bit chancier since that's around 15 to 20 years from now, and there can be all sorts of other wild changes that could happen in our world thusly shaping those future jobs.

I'll begin with jobs that various futurists have been predicting will appear in that time frame of the 2020's and the 2030's. These are jobs that I am merely reporting to you and will presumably begin to appear. You can be the judge of whether these jobs seem to make sense or not. They range quite a bit in terms of the nature of the job tasks, the opportunities that each portends, etc.

Here are a few of the predicted near-future new jobs:

- Personal Microbiome Specialist

It is said that our bodies have all sorts of bacteria that can impact how we feel and what our health consists of. Some believe that you can harness the bacteria for purposes of overcoming chronic fatigue, or to combat being overweight, and so on. A personal microbiome specialist would work with you and your physician to devise a plan of how to best deal with your personal bacteria. Likely requires a biology degree and potential certification in some medical or health related fields.

- Pharmaceutical Artisan

Legal drugs can potentially be designed for you that would be based on your genetics and other characteristics. Some say that this would be part-science and part-artistry in terms of crafting a drug combination just right for you, and it might involve examining your stem cells. This job of being a pharmaceutical artisan likely would have hefty licensing and medical training requirements.

- Memorializer

The Baby Boomers are gradually getting older and as end-of-life approaches they are presumably going to increasingly want some kind of elaborate preservation of their lives. Right now, senior citizens that had put up Facebook pages and Instagram pages that are now no longer with us aren't around anymore to do anything about those pages. A memorializer would help make arrangements to continue tributes to your life and accomplishments after you are gone.

- Organizational Disrupter

I'm sure that many of you might either want this job or believe you currently have this job. Futurists are saying that companies are at times becoming complacent and they are no longer innovating like they used to do. This could be the death knell for such companies.

This new job of being an organizational disrupter involves shaking up a firm from within, fostering risk-taking and being innovative. Good luck getting one of those jobs!

You might notice that these jobs are predicated on either advances in science or changes in society. Various advancements in the areas of the sciences, engineering, and technology are often likely to generate new jobs. Too, trends in society such as aging or firm complacency, can be the fostering agent for the emergence of new jobs.

There's something coming up in the likely 2020's and 2030's that is also sparked by advances in science, engineering, and technology, and that is anticipated will have a significant impact on society, our economy, and most of what we do.

It's the advent of AI self-driving cars.

At the Cybernetic AI Self-Driving Car Institute, we are developing AI systems for self-driving cars. We also keep track of major trends related to self-driving cars, along with making predictions about the future of AI self-driving cars, which at times includes debunking industry pundit claims.

There has already been a lot of attention paid toward the job destruction that will occur as a result of the advent of AI self-driving cars. If the AI works as hoped for by AI specialists and the auto makers, there will ultimately be no need for human drivers per se. There are an estimated 3,500,000 truck drivers in the United States alone, all of which could presumably be replaced by AI. There are an estimated 200,000 taxi drivers in the U.S., all of which could presumably be replaced by AI. There are about 2 million Uber registered drivers, and they would presumably no longer have much chance at making money as a human driver.

Keep in mind though that there is a common myth that somehow overnight we're going to be switching from human driver vehicles to AI driven vehicles. This doesn't make any sense.

There are an estimated 200+ million conventional cars in the United States and by-and-large those aren't going to be retrofitted to become AI self-driving cars. Instead, you'll need to buy a new car that is an AI self-driving car. People are not going to readily give up and discard their conventional cars for AI self-driving cars. People might not be able to readily afford an AI self-driving car, at first, though I've also mentioned many times that there are other ways in which affordability might occur.

Another aspect to keep in mind is that there are various levels of AI self-driving cars. The topmost level, which is Level 5, consists of an AI self-driving car that has no human driver involved. Indeed, the Level 5 self-driving cars are being designed to omit any brake and gas pedal, and nor would there be a steering wheel. On the other hand, the self-driving cars less than a Level 5 are still considered human driven cars. The human driver is co-sharing the driving task with the AI. There must be a human driver present in the car and the human driver is considered responsible for the actions of the self-driving car.

This is important to be aware of, due to the aspect that we'll more than likely have a range of levels of self-driving cars, and which will be a mix for many years to come. In other words, there will be some mix of conventional cars, some amount of less than Level 5 self-driving cars, and some true Level 5 self-driving cars. This mix will gradually inexorably move toward a dominance of the Level 5, but this will take years if not decades to play out.

With all the concern raised about the job losses due to AI self-driving cars, which is certainly worthy of considering and planning for, and I don't want to downplay it, but I also don't want those that seem to decry it as happening overnight to cause a false outcry, we might also consider looking a the potential of job creation due to AI self-driving cars.

It is already asserted that the advent of true AI self-driving cars will aid the shift of society towards mobility, and we're going to have a mobility-as-a-service society. This translates partially into the notion that we'll have ridesharing aplenty. You'll be able to shake a stick and voila a ridesharing car will appear. This is predicted too as a result of the AI self-driving cars being able to be used 24x7, and while you are at work your AI self-driving car will be making money doing ridesharing.

What kinds of jobs might emerge as a result of the advent of true AI self-driving cars?

Let's look into my crystal ball and see what it says (these are my predictions, right or wrong, sensible or not).

I list next some of the potentially emerging new jobs, along with an indication of the pay aspects, the skill requirements, the social skills needed, and opportunity in terms of volume of such jobs, and the career progression possibilities. I'll use a scheme of low, middle, and high for each of those job-related parameters.

These are the job parameters and their potential scoring:

- Pay: Low, Middle, High
- Technical Skill Requirements: Low, Middle, High
- Social Skill Requirements: Low, Middle, High
- Opportunity: Low, Middle, High
- Career Progression: Low, Middle, High

I'll number them for ease of reference and discussion, but it does not denote any kind of prioritization or importance factor.

With all of that introductory contextual setting, here now are the new near-term future jobs as it pertains to AI self-driving cars:

1. Self-Driving Car Chaperone

Pay: Low
Technical Skills: Low
Social Skills: Medium/High
Opportunity: High
Career Progression: Low

A true Level 5 self-driving car will be able to take your children to school, or to the baseball field, or wherever you want them to go. But, this also creates a potential issue that you'll have a car being driven by AI that has no adults in the car, and the children will be in a moving car without any adult supervision or assistance. I've written and spoken at many industry events that this is going to create new kinds of issues for us as a society.

Will the children that are unattended by an adult be locked into the self-driving car so that they cannot get out? You might say that of course you don't want the children to be able to get out of the car. Suppose though there is a need for the child to get out of the self-driving car, such as there's an emergency and the child needs to escape from the car. How will this be handled?

I realize that some say that an adult could electronically communicate with the AI of the self-driving car and be able to tell it when to unlock the doors. This presumes though that there is perfect electronic communication connections and makes other such assumptions that in the real-world are not likely to bear out, at least not all of the time.

As such, one new job would be that of a self-driving car chaperone.

This is a human being, presumably an adult, whom would ride in an AI self-driving car to accompany children and be there to help them as needed. Notice that the human does not need to know how to drive the car and does not need a driver's license. I mention this aspect because today's ridesharing services in essence do somewhat of the same service in that you have an adult driver that can "supervise" your children, but this also means that the human must be able to drive a car. That's not needed for an AI self-driving car.

Some might refer to this person as a nanny, or an au pair, or something like that. I've tended towards using the word "chaperone" since it is a word that we tend to think of as being more transitory. A nanny is someone you usually hire for an extended period of time. A chaperone you tend to think of someone hired for a particular event or situation.

There might be ridesharing services that offer AI self-driving cars and for an added fee you can have a self-driving car chaperone in the car for the journey. These would presumably be carefully screened to make sure it is appropriate that they are with children, alone, in a car.

An added kind of protection, as it were, involves that the AI self-driving car is likely to have inward facing cameras and microphones, which would allow for the recording of whatever happens while inside the AI self-driving car. Furthermore, you could be at work, connect to the AI self-driving car via your smartphone, and watch as the self-driving car takes your kids to school, along with seeing and hearing how the chaperone interacts with your children.

Undoubtedly, there would be Yelp-like ratings of the chaperones. And, rather than getting one randomly assigned to your ridesharing request, you'd likely be able to request a specific person. Thus, maybe each morning an AI self-driving car comes to your house, the chaperone you've grown to like is in the self-driving car, the kids pile into the self-driving car, and they head to school. Meanwhile, the chaperone now knows your children and the familiarity makes it easier for the children to feel comfortable about being in the AI self-driving car.

This would be a relatively low paying job and requires no technical skills. A modicum of social skills would presumably be needed. The number of such jobs could become enormous, rising as the advent of AI self-driving cars increases in popularity.

2. Self-Driving Car Consort

Pay: Low
Technical Skills: Low
Social Skills: Medium/High
Opportunity: Medium
Career Progression: Low/Medium

It is predicted that the elderly are going to become much more mobile due to emergence of AI self-driving cars. They'll be able to go where they want, when they want. This though doesn't quite provide the so-called "last mile" problem, which involves the elderly getting into the AI self-driving car and out of the AI self-driving car. Yes, there might be someone at the origination and destination to help, when needed, but this is not necessarily going to be the case. As such, it might be handy to have someone that goes along in the AI self-driving car to help out.

This also aids with the circumstance of someone that has a health-related problem arise while in an AI self-driving car, while on some kind of driving journey. If there's no human accompanying the person, and they suddenly have a heart attack, how would the AI know and what could the AI do to immediately aid the person? With another person in the AI self-driving car, they could render immediate aid, if needed.

Another potential use for a human in the AI self-driving car might be due to a delivery being made. If you order a pizza, and an AI self-driving car brings it to you, there's once again the "last mile" problem of getting the pizza from the car and up to your door.

I realize that some are saying that the human that ordered the pizza will need to come out to the self-driving car, but if you've been partying or are in your PJs, this idea of having to come out the street to grab a pizza from the self-driving car is not going to go over very well. Thus, there might be reasons to have a human delivery person in the AI self-driving car. This can be for pizza delivery, it can be for groceries delivery, you name it.

For the moment, I'm referring to this job title as a "consort" which is not entirely satisfying, and I am hoping another word will arise for this role. You could use the word "companion" but I'm not sure it fits well either. I don't think we want to use the word "escort" since it has another connotations.

You might argue that the chaperone position is similar to this one. I've purposely carved out the chaperone as a role devoted to riding in a self-driving car when there are children involved. I believe it would be prudent to make this into its own specialty. The consort is a much wider variety of circumstances. Another example of the consort would be someone that's a local tourist guide and goes with you to show you various local notable locations. And so on.

3. Self-Driving Car Auto Shop Technician

> Pay: Medium
> Technical Skills: Medium/High
> Social Skills: Low
> Opportunity: Medium
> Career Progression: Medium

AI self-driving cars are going to be chock full of specialized sensors, computer processors, and other devices that are there for purposes of making a car become an AI self-driving car. There is complicated software involved too.

This will require a specialized technician at the auto shop that is going to be doing maintenance and repairs on self-driving cars. They'll need advanced training for this.

I realize that some pundits live in a dream world wherein AI self-driving cars never break down. It is unfathomable that anyone would think that an AI self-driving car is infallible. I assure you that it is going to breakdown. They will be in accidents. Parts will go bad. Recalls will be needed. It's a car, darn it, it's a car.

4. Self-Driving Car Financier

> Pay: Medium/High
> Technical Skills: Medium
> Social Skills: Medium/High
> Opportunity: Medium
> Career Progression: Medium/High

AI self-driving cars will likely spawn thousands upon thousands of new small businesses. I say this because I've already predicted that to afford an AI self-driving car you'll likely turn it into a money making ridesharing service. If you do that, you likely will want to form a small business to be able to then deduct the costs of keeping up the AI self-driving car. There are lots of handy tax reasons to do so.

A cottage industry will form of those helping the naïve buyer of an AI self-driving car into becoming savvy about how to setup a business and do the financing involved. I'm calling this the self-driving car financier, which is kind of a fancy name for the role. If anyone has something that is better suited as a title, I welcome morphing the title. Maybe "Self-Driving Car Startup Adviser" is one such example, but it doesn't role off-the-tongue as does the simpler "Financier" does.

5. Self-Driving Car AI Add-on Developer

> Pay: High
> Technical Skills: Medium/High
> Social Skills: Low/Medium
> Opportunity: High
> Career Progression: High

AI self-driving cars are going to emerge and then become one of the biggest add-on markets that you've ever seen. The auto makers and tech firms are doing their best right now to just get the fundamental platform out into the marketplace and working. There are lots of "edge" problems that they are forsaking right now, doing so to concentrate on the core aspects.

I've predicted in my writing and at my industry presentations that once these platforms actually exist, there will be a blossoming of an add-on market. This won't be quite so easy though, because you are talking about adding onto a car which has the potential for huge safety considerations.

Developers that learn how to cope with the idiosyncrasies of particular brands of self-driving cars will be able to become specialized for that aspect. They can either be hired-on to develop add-on's on the behalf of a larger tech or auto firm, or they can make add-on's that they try to bring to the market themselves.

Right now, the size of the AI developers market for the existing auto makers and tech firms is relatively small and confined to pretty much those already known or in-the-know. Once the platform exists, there will be grand opening to developers of all kinds and capabilities. Not going to happen overnight, but it will emerge with solid job prospects.

Conclusion

There are going to be future jobs associated with the advent of AI self-driving cars. These will be new jobs that don't exist today per se. Economists and others are still pondering whether the job destruction impacts of AI self-driving cars will be greater than or the same or less than the job creation impacts. It's an ongoing debate. So far, the job destruction appears larger. But, we've not yet begun to experience the ways in which AI self-driving cars might change our society.

Note that I've not focused herein on the new jobs outside of the realm of AI self-driving cars that might arise indirectly due to the AI self-driving car. I'm sure there will be many.

For the moment, I've provided a glimpse into my crystal ball about new jobs that are directly as a result of AI self-driving cars. If you plan on working in the 2020's and 2030's, and if any of these new jobs look of interest to you or someone you know, maybe time to start planning and get a head start on being ready to step into those jobs. Happy job hunting!

CHAPTER 11

CAR WASH AND

AI SELF-DRIVING CARS

CHAPTER 11

CAR WASH AND
AI SELF-DRIVING CARS

The other day I went to my local car wash here in Southern California. After getting my car washed, I was provided with a coupon that said if it rained within the next 48 hours that I could come back for a free car wash. When I showed this to a colleague visiting here from the East Coast, he was surprised about the coupon and said he had never heard of such a thing being provided to car wash customers. I was surprised that he was surprised, since this is a pretty customary offer here in the Los Angeles area and has been as long as I can remember.

The basis for the coupon is that though we rarely get rain, there's a paltry 12 inches of rain per year and it occurs on only about 35 days of the year (meaning that 90% of the year is no rain!), the car wash businesses want to make sure that locals don't freak-out and avoid getting a car wash when there's even a chance of rain. Indeed, many here would look up at the clouds and if it looks gloomy, they might put off getting a car wash under the belief that why waste money on getting your car washed and then it gets pelted by rain and those pesky rain drops mar your shiny car. The coupon is an easy way to ensure that potential customers feel confident about getting a car wash, regardless whether rain is maybe going to occur or not.

When I was a young child, my parents had me wash our own cars as a means of earning my allowance. Rather than taking the cars to a professional car wash, they had me, the youthful amateur car washer, do so instead. It was a tedious and laborious task. Put clean water into buckets, have clean sponges and rags, be ready to wax the car after washing it, make sure to vacuum the inside of the car, and so on. I tried to make it into a game, sometimes timing myself to see how fast I could go or coming up with variant ways of doing the washing. To me, it seemed like a misuse of human labor since there were already automated car washes and I failed to see why we would not use "robotics" instead of a human to do the chore (little did I realize then that someday I would become heavily involved in AI and robots!).

Today, there are places in California that have outlawed doing car washing at your home. This also is a surprise to some out-of-towners. The basis for the law is that you might tend to waste water when washing your car, and here in parts of California we are water "starved" and required to conserve water. Presumably, a professional car wash is supposed to not only use just the right amount of water but also have provisions to reclaim the water. Furthermore, another reason that home car washes are discouraged is that the run-off from the car wash, which might include grease and oil and other contaminates, might flow into the sewer system and end-up in polluting our oceans. Professional car washes are supposed to have provisions to trap this or otherwise contend with it.

You might be wondering whether professional car washing is much of a business. We are all used to seeing car washes on various street corners and often associated with gas stations. Is there much money to be made via a car wash? Yes, indeed. In the United States alone, there are an estimated 16,000+ car wash establishments and it is estimated to be a nearly $10 billion-dollar industry, often commanding a hefty profit. Something seemingly as simple as washing cars is big business. Maybe I should have continued my amateur car washing and progressed it into a professional car wash!

The industry is dominated by smaller mom-and-pop car washes in the sense that the top 50 car washing firms only have about 20% of the total market. This means that the market is very fragmented. There isn't a handful of massive car wash firms that run things. Instead, there are lots and lots of car wash owners and car wash operators, all vying to compete with each other.

Competing can be fierce in the car wash business. Generally, the biggest competitive advantage and the one main success criteria for any car wash is its location. Car washes are considered a location-based business. People need to get their cars to your car wash. People don't want to have to go out of their way to get to the car wash. If there's a car wash a block from their home, and another one three blocks away, it's going to require something extraordinary to get those drivers to take their cars those few blocks further to get their cars washed. If you are the only car wash in-town, you've kind of got it made since the alternatives of hand washing yourself is now passé, as I've mentioned earlier.

Location is key. You still need to though have a car wash that actually does car washing. Even the best of locations can be undermined by providing shoddy car washes. People will figure this out and word will spread. Other than unsuspecting drivers, you won't get any repeat business. You need to leverage a good location and make sure that you provide sufficient quality and consistency of your car washes.

Of course, in case your car wash and another one is pretty close in terms of location, you can try to differentiate your car wash. They all pretty much need to be able to wash, clean, and wax, in terms of the services being provided. Those are the basics needed to be playing the game, the so-called table stakes. Time is an important factor for most customers, and so the faster your car wash can complete the service, the better it is perceived. But, you cannot sacrifice the basics for the speed, in the sense that even if you are a faster washer, if the end result is a car not as clean as some other slightly slower car wash, the odds are that people will figure this out and no longer consider your faster speed of much value.

Here's what the mantra of car washes is, and for which people expect and clamor for out of a car wash: Clean, dry, and shiny.

This can be achieved by providing a hands-off automated service operation. People drive up their cars, usually enter a code to activate the car wash, drive forward into the car wash, remain in their cars as the car gets washed and waxed, and then proceed out of the car wash when finished. These are the tunnel systems that have become prevalent at most car washes. There are also the full-service operations, consisting of labor that will drive your car forward for you, and do hand drying and vacuuming inside of your car. Most car washes choose one or the other of the two approaches.

One means to gain some added revenue and profit involves selling merchandise at the car wash. The full-service car washes especially do this since the human driver usually gets out of their car and has nothing much else to do while the car is being washed. Might as well see if the car wash can make some more bucks off those idle customers. This though also ups the ante on the nature of the experience for the customer. If a customer interacts with a scowling retail clerk, the customer might decide to never come back to the car wash, even though the car wash itself might be doing a wonderful job washing cars.

Speaking of labor, the automated operations have reduced the labor that used to be involved in car washing. There are some that cling to the belief that the labor-based full-service car washes are much better than the automated no-labor ones, but overall the market has shown that the "express" washes have grown like weeds and obviously have satisfied a significant segment of the market.

Car washes will try to encourage loyalty by offering various loyalty cards or clubs to customers. Purchase five car washes and get the sixth one free. Some go the subscription route, wherein you buy a year's worth of car washes or maybe even unlimited number of annual car washes. There can also be discounts and special programs involved. Veterans get a 10% discount. Or, if your child goes to the local high school, you get a discount on your car wash.

So, in recap, we seem to really want to have our cars washed, as evidenced by the billion dollar industry of professional car washing. Car washing is more than just a idle concept, it's a big business and one that consumers seem to relish.

What does this have to do with AI self-driving cars?

At the Cybernetic AI Self-Driving Car Institute, we are developing AI systems for self-driving cars. One of the "edge" problems involves how AI self-driving cars can handle car washes.

When I refer to an edge problem, it means a type of problem not considered at the core of an otherwise larger problem. In the case of AI self-driving cars, being able to have the AI drive a car is at the core of the driving task. You want to make sure that the AI can properly undertake the driving while the car is on the highway, doing so while in the inner-city areas, and while in the suburbs, etc. That's the mainstay of the driving tasks for the AI.

Having the AI be able to properly navigate and undertake a car wash is admittedly quite a bit further down on the list of priorities. Nonetheless, it is an interesting problem and one that obviously provides some value to car owners, given the rather sizable nature of the car washing industry. Imagine if you have a brand-new shiny AI self-driving car, but it cannot make its way into and through a car wash. This would seem like a let-down and in fact suggest that the AI is rather weak that it cannot handle something as simple as contending with a car wash. I've previously written about how the same thing can apply to other areas of driving tasks, such as being able to handle tolls at bridges.

The car wash industry would certainly want to be able to tap into doing car washes for AI self-driving cars. There are an estimated 200+ million conventional cars today in the United States, and presumably ultimately, they will be overtaken by AI self-driving cars. It won't happen overnight. And, it is most likely that the AI self-driving cars will be new purchases, rather than somehow retrofitting the existing conventional cars. But, if somehow it is difficult or arduous to get AI self-driving cars to enter into and get car washed, this would not be good for the car wash industry.

This point about the AI self-driving cars being new purchases ties again to the topic of car washes in another facet. The newer the car, the more likely that consumers take their car to the car wash. The older the car, the less likely they take their car to the car wash. This makes sense when you ponder it for a moment. If I have new shiny car, I want it to look new and shiny, and be able to show it off and enjoy the newness of it. If I have an older somewhat beat-up car, scratches included and other divots, it probably wouldn't matter much to me whether it looks new and shiny. In fact, I suppose the dirt and grime might help to hide the aspect that it is an older and somewhat downtrodden car.

With the gradual sunsetting of conventional cars, people will likely not go to car washes as much. No need to take in your conventional car that's becoming gradually and progressively outdated.

With the advent of AI self-driving cars, since those are generally going to be new cars, people will likely want to go to car washes again. Therefore, over time, the car wash industry will see quite an impact of the decreasing interest by consumers of washing their conventional cars, and presumably an arising and increasing interest in getting their AI self-driving cars washed.

There are other factors that might further boost the car washing industry as a result of the advent of AI self-driving cars. One is that it is anticipated that most AI self-driving cars will be turned into ridesharing services. This makes sense in that if you have a self-driving car that can be driving 24x7, and if you can make money by renting it out, you would likely do so. In that sense, AI self-driving cars will need to look nice, presumably, as a means of appearing attractive to the ridesharing public, and also with the self-driving cars being on-the-go 24x7 there's heightened chances of them getting dirty or at least dirty looking.

Could be good times for car washes!

Those AI self-driving cars that are involved in ridesharing might be coming to car washes with a high frequency. This keeps the AI self-driving car looking in good shape. And, since the AI self-driving car is on-the-road a lot, it will likely need to get car washed with a higher frequency than today's conventional cars. As an analogy, some sales people that drive their cars all day long here in Los Angeles area tend to get their cars washed several times a week, wanting to keep the car looking shiny and also to deal with the dust and grime that gets onto their always being driven cars.

Let's go ahead and assume therefore that there will be interest in having AI self-driving cars go to the car wash. I think we can all agree to that notion. You might quibble about the frequency aspects, but in any case, it seems reasonable to believe that owners of AI self-driving cars will want to get those cars washed, from time-to-time or for a lot of the time.

What's the big deal, you might ask, it's a car and its getting washed. End of story.

Not so fast! We can dig further into this topic.

First, I'd bet that the times of day that an AI self-driving car will be going to a car wash might differ overall than today's conventional cars. Think about that for a moment. Today's conventional cars require that a human driver take the car to the car wash. This generally means that the time chosen is a time best suited to the human driver. I might have a lunch break and use that time to take my car to the car wash. I might do so after work, or on the weekend.

In the case of the AI self-driving car, for a true Level 5 self-driving car, which is one that can drive without any human driver on-board the car, the AI self-driving car can be sent to the car wash at the bidding of the car owner. This can happen any time of the day. If I were ridesharing out my AI self-driving car, I would likely want to have it fully available during the prime time of when people need a ridesharing pick-up. It wouldn't make sense for me to send my AI self-driving car to the car wash when it could otherwise be making me money by doing ridesharing.

So, the odds are that I'd send my AI self-driving car to the car wash at oddball times, such as say 3:00 a.m. when presumably there is little or no ridesharing opportunities occurring. This means that car wash owners need to realize that they might see a radical shift of when cars come to their car washes. If you are a labor-based car wash, you might need to reconsider the work shifts of your labor. If you are a fully automated car wash, this change in times might not impact your labor, but it also means that your car wash is going to be in higher use at oddball times, and if it breaks down or needs maintenance, that's going to happen at oddball times too.

Another facet of AI self-driving cars and car washes will be the likelihood that there is no human occupant in the self-driving car when it arrives at the car wash. This means that the car wash itself cannot rely upon a human being to aid in the process of having the car proceed into and undertake the car wash. It's going to be done entirely with the AI system of the self-driving car.

This lends itself to technological related solutions.

The car wash might be outfitted with Internet of Things (IoT) devices that can readily electronically communicate with the AI self-driving car. This would allow the AI and the car wash to engage in an electronic dialogue about what needs to be done. It's almost like having an air-traffic-controller that can guide the self-driving car, such as move to the front of the tunnel, move forward onto the conveyer belt, stop now that you are on the conveyer belt, and so on.

For those car washes that won't modernize, the AI could try to do the same things that human drivers do today. This often involves reading signs that describe what to do. The AI could use its sensors to try and figure out where the self-driving car needs to be placed within the washing system. This can be trickier than it seems since if the AI places the self-driving car to the left or right of some obstruction, it could end-up hit the self-driving car. If you've ever driven into an automated car wash, you likely know the "dance" involved of you maneuvering the car and the car wash trying to crudely convey to you where the car needs to be (sometimes they flash lights, sometimes they blare a horn).

The effort by the AI to contend with a "dumb" car wash is going to be much greater than a modernized "smart" car wash that can electronically use IoT or the equivalent. As such, those car washes that are slow to modernize might find themselves as a disadvantage in terms of attracting owners of AI self-driving cars not wanting to send their cars to the outdated car wash.

This brings up another significant point about the fundamental nature of car washes, which I've mentioned earlier is their location.

Will location of a car wash still matter in a world of AI self-driving cars?

You might say that it won't be as important anymore. The AI self-driving car can be sent to wherever the owner opts to send it. This is a factor that will no longer depend on the human driver. We usually go to a car wash near our home or work place. With an AI self-driving car, the owner of the self-driving car can just tell it to go to anyplace that the owner thinks is best to have the car get washed.

It could be that the owner of an AI self-driving car will want to keep it mainly in a geographical area that has the best odds of getting ridesharing. If they are also using it for personal driving purposes, they'd obviously still want the AI self-driving car to come to their home and their workplace. In that sense, there's some hope for car wash locations of today in that the owners might still want to have the car washed near their home or workplace. But, this is not something quite as guaranteed as it is with today's conventional cars.

Another facet of car washes will be whether or not they are able to accommodate the physical aspects of an AI self-driving car. The versions of AI self-driving cars that are being utilized today tend to have a LIDAR system on the top of the car, and have various sensitive cameras, radar, sonic sensors that are embedded just under the skin of the car or sometimes mounted on the exterior of the self-driving car.

If you drive an AI self-driving car into a conventional car wash, the ones that have the various brushes and aren't touchless, the question will be whether the AI self-driving car will survive the car wash. It could be that the lenses might get scratched or some sensors might be sheered off. A car wash that wants to attract AI self-driving cars will need to make sure it can accommodate any of the physical considerations associated with an AI self-driving car.

This also brings up whether the car wash will also be doing anything inside of the AI self-driving car.

I would tend to think car washes would perceive the interior cleaning aspects to be a good potential money maker. Here's why. If you are using your AI self-driving car for ridesharing, and someone drunkenly upchucks while in your AI self-driving car, as the owner you probably don't want to deal directly with cleaning up the mess, and so instead you would likely route your AI self-driving car to the nearest car wash that can provide that kind of cleaning service.

It would seem like an owner of an AI self-driving car is likely to consider using car washes to help keep the interior of the car clean. This is good news for the car washes. It could be that you might need to route your AI self-driving car to the car wash every day, just to keep it cleaned-up after all the people that have ridden in your self-driving car throughout the day have dirtied it. As owner of the self-driving car, you could do the cleaning yourself, but I'd bet that most AI self-driving car owners would aim to have a car wash do it, if the price is right.

I can imagine that car washes will provide a range of specialized services for AI self-driving cars. This could be a key differentiator as to why an owner sends their self-driving car to car wash X versus car wash Y.

Some added twists will be that the car owner can presumably be monitoring the car wash while their AI self-driving car is at one. Via the cameras on the AI self-driving car, the owner could presumably on their smartphone bring up what the self-driving car sees and watch as the car wash undertakes the services requested. There are likely inward facing cameras too, and thus when the car wash has someone doing cleaning inside of the self-driving car, the owner can watch that too.

Not only could the owner watch what is happening, they presumably can interact too with whomever is at the car wash. For the inside cleaning of a car, right now it's mainly a manual effort. The outside cleaning can be readily automated, but the interior cleaning is not so easily automated. As such, assuming that the car wash has labor that goes into the AI self-driving car to clean it, the owner can watch what is being done and likely even interact with the labor (hey, you missed a spot right there on the backseat, please wipe it again).

Another aspect could be the scheduling of having an AI self-driving car go to a car wash. I'm sure you've had moments where you drove to a car wash and there were several cars ahead of you. You had to either wait it out, or decide to come back. With an AI self-driving car, if it's being used for other purposes such as ridesharing, having it sit at a car wash waiting to get washed is not a good use of its time. Therefore, a "smart" car wash would likely put in place an electronically scheduling system.

An AI self-driving car could communicate over the Internet with a car wash scheduling system and indicate that it wants to come to the car wash in twenty minutes and make an appointment to do so. This could be done via the same mechanism on-board the AI self-driving car for doing OTA (Over the Air) updates.

There might even be the use of blockchain for keeping track of car washes undertaken by AI self-driving cars and be used to aid in the electronic payment for the use of the car wash. All in all, there are a myriad of ways in which automation can make the entire life cycle of seeking a car wash to going there to then getting washed, entirely be something that requires no particular human intervention.

The famous song by Rose Royce about car washes relates that you might not ever get rich working at a car wash, but it's at least better than digging a ditch. Generally, the already reduced use of labor at car washes is likely to continue, though until there's an automated solution for cleaning of the interior of a car (a robot?), there's still some amount of labor required. In any case, the advent of AI self-driving cars will not do away with the need for car washes and to the contrary would seem to bolster the need for car washes. For those out there that are thinking of investing in a car wash, it seems like a reasonably good bet, but you'll need to be willing to modernize your car wash for it to be well-aligned with the needs of AI self-driving cars and the human owners of those self-driving cars. See you at the car wash!

CHAPTER 12
5G AND
AI SELF-DRIVING CARS

CHAPTER 12

5G AND
AI SELF-DRIVING CARS

Repeat after me, there's 1G, and 2G, and 3G and more, plus 4G today and 5G is galore! I wax poetic about the future because 5G is on all our minds and we wait breathlessly for it to arrive. For those of you that are desirous of speed and have that incurable itch to get the fastest streaming you can find, I'm sure you are watching closely the upcoming emergence of 5G.

The Fifth Generation (5G) of wireless technology is about as big a deal as the invention of writing and the creation of fire. The telecommunications companies are incessantly teasing us with the prospects of what 5G can provide. You've likely seen ads that tout speeds at 100-times that of 4G, or maybe 30-times that of 4G, or some more sober writings that say it might be just 4-times 4G, or perhaps even slower than 4G. Say what? How can there be so many interpretations of what the speed difference is going to be?

Part of the problem is that the standard for 5G is still somewhat loosey goosey. Another problem is that just like for a car and MPG (Miles Per Gallon), as they say your mileage can vary, and so is the case for 5G. One setup for 5G can be materially different in performance from another. Generally, 5G architecturally makes use of the IEEE 802.11ac wireless networking standard and should, in theory, be a boost over the 4G standard of IEEE 802.11n. Generally, it is claimed that 5G will be around 10-20 Gigabits per second (Gbps), while traditional 4G is perhaps around 100 Mbps, and 3G is around 384 Kbps. The proof though of actual 5G speeds will be in the pudding.

If we can really get the speed performance hoped for, you'll see all sorts of exciting changes. The most obvious ones would be that you can do Virtual Reality (VR) and Augmented Reality (AR) in a manner that is not especially feasible nowadays due to the slower wireless speeds of today. It is said that medical doctors will be able to perform surgeries remotely since the 5G speed will allow them to operate on a patient as though they were right there in the operating room with them. The Internet of Things (IoT) will shift from being a kind of novelty to becoming ubiquitous due to the 5G capability of making those portable wireless connected IoT devices more real-time capable in the receiving and sending of data.

5G is such a big deal that countries are fighting over the posturing of who will get there first. In the eyes of many, it's primarily a China versus the United States kind of battle. Two titans, each wanting to get to 5G. Each expecting that it will transform their society. Each wanting not only the substance of advantages by 5G, but also the bragging rights too. It's kind of like the Cold War era bragging over getting to outer space or perhaps even to the moon.

Some would say that China is already ahead of the United States. By leveraging its rather all-encompassing government control, China has seemingly gotten a massive alignment among its constituents, including the Chinese government, tech firms, businesses, and the like, all sharing the same 5G fever. Others would say that the United States, in spite of its more "freewheeling" approach to adopting 5G (some might say chaotic), will end-up getting there soonest as the all-mighty dollar is a sure means of creating momentum. These two horses on the race track are at times each perhaps slightly ahead or behind the other, but it seems a bit premature to be calling the race just yet.

Not all though is rosy about 5G. The city of Mill Valley, just outside of San Francisco and not far from the denizens of Silicon Valley, recently passed an ordinance to block or ban 5G from getting established there. Why would they stop the advent of such great wireless speed? Are they luddites? They assert that there are potential health and safety concerns. You recall the ongoing debate about whether holding a cell phone to your ear can cause potential bad health consequences? Some believe that 5G might do something similar.

Part of why those concerned about 5G are troubled is that the path to 5G involves setting up lots and lots of small-cell 5G transmitters. The large towers that were put in place to get us to the 3G and 4G world are not what's going to make 5G a reality per se. Instead, 5G will be mainly dependent on relatively small 5G transmitter devices that are going to be placed everywhere feasible. The good news is that their small size means that you can put them just about anywhere and you might not especially notice they are there. They'll be on lampposts, on rooftops, on walls, on billboards, and so on.

There's a word you ought to know to be techno-savvy about 5G, namely densify. If your normal vocabulary does not include the word "densify" that's OK, since it is currently rarely used (soon, it will be a popular word!). It means to make something dense or compressed. The way that 5G works is that it generally can only go somewhat short distances and so you'll need lots of them in a given area to have it work appropriately (they use higher frequency waves, while the 4G and 3G use lower frequency waves which can normally go further). Densification is coming. The telecommunications firms are going to want to put up the 5G communications devices on every inch and corner of where people are going to want 5G.

One of the biggest questions beyond the health and safety involves the cost factor. How much will 5G cost us? It's going to take a lot of very costly technology infrastructure to get 5G put into place. The telecommunications firms are going to want to recoup those costs. There's also the likelihood that the ongoing upkeep costs of 5G will be high, partially due the numerous 5G devices that will be laborious to keep functioning and repair/replace.

If the cost of 5G is "outlandish" then it will take some really pressing ROI (return on investment) to get someone to pay for it. It might be overly pricey for the everyday person to use 5G. Could be that only businesses with big bucks will be able to afford it. Of course, like any new technology, the odds are that as 5G becomes more pervasive, and with the competition gradually becoming more prevalent, we'll see the pricing come down. Recall that when cell phones first appeared, it was a rarity to see one and only a select segment of society could afford it (remember, people used to wear it on their belt and it was considered a novelty and a conversation starter!). Now, we all seem to have cell phones and use them to our hearts content.

For the moment, let's put aside the cost factor and assume that we'll have "affordable" 5G at some point (I'm not underplaying the cost aspects, just want to put it to the side for a moment to cover other facets, but please do keep in mind that cost will ultimately come to play in 5G, at least for sure when it starts emerging).

At a high-level strategic viewpoint, the main thing about 5G to be considering is that it will:

- Provide high bandwidth

- Involving faster speeds

- With more data at the same time

- Having a low latency (less delay)

- Using lower electrical power

If you have some kind of need for exchanging small sized packets of data, doing so very quickly, and without much delay, you ought to be considering 5G since that's a sweet spot for it. 5G is supposed to provide sub one-millisecond latency, which is a nifty improvement in reducing latency.

Where might this kind of capability be needed?

I'd like to tell you about AI self-driving cars.

At the Cybernetic AI Self-Driving Car Institute, we are developing AI systems for self-driving cars. We also keep tabs on the latest high-tech trends and are determined to include any viable new-tech advances into the development of self-driving cars.

One such new high-tech is the emergence of 5G.

To consider how 5G might make a difference for AI self-driving cars, you need to consider what kinds of electronic communication needs might an AI self-driving car have.

Let's start with the OTA (Over The Air) updates for an AI self-driving car. Most of the auto makers and tech firms that are developing AI self-driving cars are making use of their own specialized cloud capabilities to be able to electronically communicate with their AI self-driving cars. Each such company is taking slightly different approaches, and so right now there's not one super grand universal cloud for all AI self-driving cars (and, some doubt there ever will be, while others suggest that there should be, presumably as a means to have all AI self-driving cars learn from each other, but this also begs privacy and Big Brother issues).

The OTA capability allows for both the uploading of data from the AI self-driving car and also the downloading of data and programs.

While the AI self-driving car is driving around, it is collecting all sorts of data from its myriad of sensors, including camera pictures and video, radar data, sonic data, LIDAR data, and so on. This can potentially be uploaded to the cloud. From this uploaded data, the auto maker or tech firm could use it for a multitude of purposes. One such purpose would be to use it for Machine Learning (ML) and try to improve the performance of their AI self-driving cars accordingly.

Another purpose would be to use it for analyzing driving patterns, such as where people go, how long it takes, etc. This could be used for purposes of improving our roadways and might be shared with certain governmental bodies. The data could also be used for business purposes such as being able to let retailers know how often you drive near to their establishment. There's likely a treasure trove of data that could be either sold to third-party firms or analyzed for them. Money is likely to be found via the nature of the data collected. Whether the public will want this, or stand for it, we'll need to wait and see.

The OTA also can download to the AI self-driving car. This is perhaps the most touted feature of the OTA. When your AI self-driving car needs an update to the software on-board, you won't need to go to a local dealership to physically have an automobile mechanic load it. Instead, via OTA, the latest updates will be beamed into your AI self-driving car. This can be quite handy and would allow for your AI self-driving car to be updated with the latest Machine Learning results that the auto maker or tech firm has found, or add new features into the software, or fix bugs or errors that exist in the software.

Generally, the OTA is most likely to take place on a "batch update" oriented basis. In other words, right now, we're all pretty much assuming that the OTA will happen when there's a time and place available to do so. Some of the AI self-driving cars require that OTA only occur when the self-driving car is unmoving and parked. You would tend to think of this like an EV (electrical vehicle) which gets charged when it is unmoving and parked. Likewise, the OTA updates would normally occur when you AI self-driving car is perhaps parked at home in your garage, or maybe when it is parked at work.

Part of the reason for doing the OTA on a batch-oriented basis is due to the electronic communication needed with the AI self-driving car. Trying to electronically communicate with an AI self-driving car that's going 75 miles per hour on the freeway is likely problematic. The connection is bound to be spotty, slow, and get disrupted. Instead, waiting until the self-driving car is in a nice quiet place and not underway would seem handier.

There are other factors involved too, such as even if the OTA could happen while the AI self-driving car is in motion, it would seem untoward to consider making updates to the on-board AI system during it's crucial efforts of driving the car. You might be willing to download updates to the AI self-driving car, but you'd be safest to wait to actually have those updates installed, doing so when the AI is otherwise unoccupied with keeping your car on the road and you safe from getting killed.

The 5G can help out with the OTA.

The amount of time required to upload or download data from the cloud to the AI self-driving car could be lengthy under a 4G or 3G scenario. The hope is that 5G will be much faster and therefore the OTA time will be lessened. We don't know how long it's going to take to normally do OTA on an ongoing basis for most AI self-driving cars, but at slower wireless speeds of today and possibly with large updates being downloaded or the voluminous data being uploaded, it could presumably at times take hours to do (5G faster speeds might reduce it to minutes).

So, score one point for 5G on helping out with OTA for AI self-driving cars.

There's another way in which 5G might help.

We pretty much assume that people will start riding in their cars a lot when they have an AI self-driving car. It's going to be handy to have an electronic chauffer that will drive you wherever you want to go. When you drive to work in the morning, your hour-long driving commute will no longer involve you driving the car and so you'll have that hour to do something else instead. I suppose you could take a nap, but maybe instead you'll want to be entertained, such as streaming the latest baseball game underway or watching a movie that's just been released. Or, maybe you'll use the time to take an online college course.

Also, AI self-driving cars are going to boost ridesharing. People will turn their AI self-driving car into a money-making machine. While they are at work, they'll be renting out their AI self-driving car. While people are sleeping, they will rent out their AI self-driving car. We're heading toward a mobility-as-a-service economy. When consumers opt to take your AI self-driving car for a ride, what will they do while inside your AI self-driving car? One answer is that they might like to be entertained by having streaming video or audio.

All of that in-car "live" entertaining requires electronic communication. Of course, you could have pre-stored movies or other pre-taped material instead, but I'd bet that humans will want fresh and live content while in an AI self-driving car. With the advent of 5G, it will make that streaming even more glorious. At the speeds of 3G and 4G, the streaming might be rather stilted and broken. The hope is that 5G would make it seem smooth and watchable.

We now though need to consider the reality of how that 5G is going to happen.

If your AI self-driving car is parked at the office or at home in your garage, the use of 5G is going to be quite likely and thus the OTA will be fine. It would make sense that you'll likely have 5G transmitters in your home, or at the office. But, the live streaming of entertainment and other such video and audio, while the AI self-driving car is in motion, that's going to be tricky to arrange. Recall that I mentioned the 5G goes usually only short distances. How will that happen while you are cruising on the freeway?

The odds are that we'll need to have lots and lots of 5G devices placed along our major highways and byways. Thus, as the AI self-driving car is rocketing down that freeway, it is moving right near and past a 5G transmitter and another one and another one. This will require some clever handling of hand-offs from device to device and still keep the moving car connected in any fluid fashion. This tough problem does though seem technologically feasible and can ultimately be worked out.

Besides in-car entertainment, AI self-driving cars are likely to have a zillion Internet of Things (IoT) devices either included into the self-driving car by the auto maker, or by having been added-in, or by human occupants that carry into the self-driving car their IoT devices such as their fitness wristband, their IoT connected jewelry, their smartphone, their tablet, etc. The 5G capability, once again via lots of transmitters along the roadside, would allow those IoT devices to ping and play.

Here's another way in which 5G can help, and it actually deals with the driving of the self-driving car.

AI self-driving cars are likely to have V2V (vehicle-to-vehicle) communication capabilities. This will allow one AI self-driving car to electronically chat with another AI self-driving car. Suppose there's an AI self-driving car a mile up ahead of your AI self-driving car, and it has spotted a car accident. It could communicate to your AI self-driving car and forewarn it about the accident. Your AI self-driving car might then start to slow down or maybe take an alternative route that goes around the accident scene.

This V2V capability is still being worked out. There are evolving protocols about what is communicated and how it is communicated. We need to deal with the dangers of false V2V that tries to trick an AI self-driving car. There's also the concern that a DoS (denial of service) type of attack could happen by someone swamping your AI self-driving car with tons of meaningless messages via V2V. But, anyway, the other factor is how will the V2V electronic communication actually take place.

One approach is that the V2V could be done not just directly from one vehicle to another, but maybe it first goes to a 5G device near the roadside, which then relays it to the destination car that's nearby. Thus, the AI self-driving cars could be bouncing their electronic messages off of the 5G devices near the roadside and then other AI self-driving cars could be picking up those messages.

This also brings up the rise of V2I (vehicle-to-infrastructure). We'll gradually be having our roadway infrastructure outfitted to be "smart" in the sense that a bridge might be able to electronically transmit that it is overly crowded and to be avoided. Or, the traffic signal at the intersection near your home might send out an electronic signal, which would be handy for an AI self-driving car, rather than solely being dependent on displaying a green-yellow-red light. AI self-driving cars will be seeking out the V2I data so as to properly route the self-driving car and be able to avoid traffic jams or more align with traffic conditions.

Once again, 5G could help out.

When I say that 5G might be able to help with the V2V and V2I, it is especially notable that we're talking about 5G because of the low latency involved. It's one thing to transmit an electronic message, but if there's a delay in it getting received, the delay time with an AI self-driving car could be crucial. A split second might make the difference between the AI making a determination to brake the self-driving car and avoid a terrible accident. If the transmission is coming from a 3G or 4G transmitter versus a 5G, the latency could be the difference between life and death.

We might have more than just a slew of 5G transmitters scattered throughout our roadways. We might also have some serious computing power that's also nearby the roadways. This is referred to as "edge computing" and it's a somewhat new trend toward putting computer processing closer to wherever the action is.

In the case of AI self-driving cars, the notion for edge computing is that an AI self-driving car might be able to do more of a real-time interaction with the auto maker or tech firm cloud if it had the processing and data sitting closer to where the AI self-driving car is (in this case, zipping along on the highway).

You might want to keep your eye on the work being done by VTT Technical Research Centre of Finland and being done with Nokia, in which they are doing tests and trials of using 5G with self-driving cars and edge computing. Using the VTT self-driving car called Martti, they are doing some interesting explorations on a vehicle test track in Sodankyla. The 5G though is still in prototype stages and thus we'll need to wait and see what happens once they've got some "real" 5G to tryout. They are also experimenting with being able to dynamically select whatever radio signal is actually available, meaning that if 5G is available it uses 5G, but if only 4G is available it contends with 4G, and so on. The overall project, known as 5G-Safe, involves considering autonomous driving along with time-critical aspects while the car is on the move.

When you think about an AI self-driving car, it's helpful to be aware of the levels of self-driving cars. A true self-driving car is considered Level 5, it's the topmost ranking of a self-driving car and refers to the aspect that there is no need for a human driver. Indeed, there's usually no brake pedal and no gas pedal, and no steering wheel. Self-driving cars at less than a Level 5 are expected and must still have a human driver present and so also have the pedals and steering wheel in the car. In the less than Level 5 self-driving cars, there is a kind of co-sharing of the driving task, which has some significant disadvantages and provides inherent dangers.

In theory, an AI self-driving car of a Level 5 is considered fully autonomous. It requires no human driver.

Please be aware that some are stretching this a bit by providing a remote "pilot" human driver in case the AI goes awry or gets stuck, but I'd dare say that most purists would contend this is not a true Level 5 per se and not fully autonomous, not at least in the sense that it is able to drive the car without any human intervention needed.

Some assert that using a remote human "pilot" is a bad idea overall, since it really is just a crutch and won't motivate us as AI developers into fully developing the AI be a truly fluent and self-sufficient driver of a car.

Let's though put aside for the moment the notion of a remote human "pilot" and pretend it is out of scope for this discussion.

This brings us to one of the more interesting and challenging questions about an AI self-driving car, namely whether it should be entirely autonomous with respect to itself, or whether it is OK to consider having it interact with other AI that might not be on-board of the self-driving car (AI that is "off-board"), doing so in the act of actually driving the car.

Allow me to elaborate.

Suppose your AI self-driving car is going along on the freeway. It's doing its thing and driving the car just fine. It's a Level 5 self-driving car. There are no humans involved in the driving task. All of a sudden, right there in the middle of the freeway a family of ducks is waddling along (this really happened here in Southern California recently – you'll be relieved to know that the ducks survived, and no humans were hurt in the process of avoiding the ducklings).

Anyway, the AI of this particular self-driving car has perhaps never before encountered ducks on the freeway. What should it do? It might have some general principles to fall back onto such as don't hit objects on the freeway. It might try to compare the images of the ducks to other images of animals, such as dogs and cats, which perhaps it's Machine Learning had already figured out what dogs and cats look like and act like. But, the ML ascertains merely that these ducks don't seem to be dogs or cats.

The AI might have then some generalized plan that if there is a series of moving objects, and they aren't identifiable per se, it should try to avoid them. This though might be tempered by the aspect that if the objects are small, and if avoiding them might be a risky maneuver, it is permitted to run over the objects, which is perhaps the safest choice in some cases. For example, if a tumbleweed is blowing across the freeway, it might be safer to strike the tumbleweed than it is to suddenly come to a halt or make a dangerous swerve to avoid it.

Under the logic that these are small objects, and that they are comparable to tumbleweeds, the AI might determine that the "right" course of action involves running over the ducks. Horrid! Can you imagine the headlines: "AI Quackery Smacks and Kills Ducks on Freeway" (or something like that).

Here's a possible alternative. The AI of the self-driving car, being somewhat stumped about these small objects, opts to seek out a second opinion. It opens an electronic connection with a nearby edge computing device, doing so via 5G, and shares with the computing device what it knows about the objects. This computing device, placed there by the auto maker or tech firm that made the AI system of the self-driving car, quickly looks up and discovers that ducks have been seen before and thus it knows what to do about ducks on the freeway. It shares this piece of "knowledge" with the on-board AI system and the AI self-driving opts to avoid hitting the ducks. The ducks are saved!

We have then three kinds of autonomous AI self-driving cars:

- Standalone autonomous

- Exo-dependent autonomous

- Exo-augmented autonomous

The standalone autonomous is an AI self-driving car that is not setup to do any kind of AI-to-AI related co-sharing of the driving task. It is entirely standalone. No phone an AI-friend possibility.

The exo-dependent autonomous is an AI self-driving car that uses an external AI-capability to help undertake the driving task, and for which the AI self-driving car is dependent upon the external AI to be available. In other words, the external AI is vital to the driving task and the AI of the self-driving car is not standalone autonomous. There are driving situations for which the on-board AI must have access to the external AI in order to perform the driving task.

The exo-augmented autonomous is an AI self-driving car that uses an external AI-capability to help undertake the driving task, but the on-board AI doesn't necessarily need the outside help. It will use it if the help is available, and give it due consideration, but otherwise even without the outside AI assistance the on-board AI is able to undertake the driving task.

Keep in mind that the exo-dependent and exo-augmented variants seem like the remote "piloting" that I mentioned earlier, but this is not quite the case because the conventional notion of remote "piloting" is that a human is the remote pilot. In the truly autonomous AI self-driving car, we're still keeping the human out of the picture, and instead simply saying that we might distribute out the AI.

In the example of the ducks on the freeway, the AI self-driving car opted to use the localized edge computing that had local-AI pertinent to this particular AI system. We'll assume in this situation that the on-board AI of the self-driving car was of the exo-augmented autonomous style, and could have proceeded without having accessed the off-board AI. Sadly, if the on-board AI had not opted to consult the off-board AI, and in this example, it might have cost the ducks their lives. But, I don't want you to assume that just because there's an off-board AI that it means the off-board AI will always somehow save the day.

You could argue that the off-board AI might make things worse, at times. It could be that the off-board AI makes a determination that if it had not been consulted then the on-board AI would have made the "right" choice. It could also be that the use of the off-board AI chewed up time, during which the on-board AI, if it had made a choice sooner, would have been better off, rather than having waited until the off-board AI was consulted.

Trying to distribute out the AI of the AI self-driving car is only going to be viable if you have very high speeds and very low latency. Any significant delay of the on-board AI to the off-board AI, and back from the off-board AI to the on-board AI, kind of undermines the whole deal. You might be able to use the off-board AI for broader planning purposes, but any kind of in-the-moment needs would not be viable unless you have the appropriate electronic communication capability, which might well be 5G.

I'd like to also point out that we can extend the distributed AI aspects to include the other nearby AI self-driving cars. I had mentioned before the V2V aspects of AI self-driving cars. Presumably, the on-board AI of the self-driving car could have potentially asked another AI self-driving car a question about the object on the freeway. It is quite possible that another brand of AI self-driving car might have already known about ducks, and so it could have told the upcoming AI self-driving car what they are and offered a suggestion of what to do.

5G, it is a galore. Exciting times are a coming. For AI self-driving cars, it bodes well that 5G is emerging. With it, the nature of the OTA speed and timing might be dramatically improved. The in-car entertainment and use of IoT might be vastly improved. The federated or distributed AI might be feasible, becoming so because of 5G. It's handy timing that just as AI self-driving cars are getting to a stage of reasonable feasibility, so too will 5G be coming along. They are two brothers, each aiding the other (5G obviously can enhance AI self-driving cars, and a justification for 5G would be that AI self-driving cars can be enabled or improved via the advent of 5G).

Let's be clear though that 5G is still being developed and implemented. We don't know how good it will be. We can't say how long it will take to get perfected. And, it will certainly be costly to put it in place, especially if you are anticipating having squillions of them lined along our freeways and highways.

Let's not hold our breath for 5G. All the work on AI self-driving cars should be proceeding for now under the assumption there is no 5G per se. That being said, we should be working towards the next iteration of AI self-driving cars, wherein 5G is available. And, dare I say, we can even start on designs of AI self-driving cars of the further future that will use 6G. I know it's a bit farfetched to already have my eye on 6G, but hey, it's never to early to start planning for the future. Soon enough, 5G will become tiresome and worn out, and we'll be all signing the praises of 6G.

CHAPTER 13

GEN Z AND

AI SELF-DRIVING CARS

CHAPTER 13

GEN Z AND

AI SELF-DRIVING CARS

Which gen are you?

Maybe you are a Baby Boomer, having been born sometime around 1946 to 1964, and having grown-up during a time when there has generally been good prosperity in the United States. In the news, you hear about the Millennials, born generally around 1980 to 1994, and were allegedly spoiled by their helicopter parents of the Baby Boomer era, always watching over their children and pampering them.

It is often said that those "spoiled" millennials seem to think that they are special, and the world owes them something (hey, I'm not making such accusations, it's what is being reported about Millennials!). Some companies have claimed that millennials aren't willing to put in a day's full work. Millennials supposedly insist that they want to have a life outside work, and so put work as a secondary priority in their busy lives. Meanwhile, purportedly Baby Boomers were the workhorses and look at disdain at a younger generation that doesn't seem to think that they need to do whatever it takes to make a career.

I am somewhat loath to make such generalizations about the generations. I certainly know many Baby Boomers that are not the all-vaunted will kill to get and keep a job, and likewise I know a lot of Millennials that take their careers very seriously and routinely put in 60 to 80 hour weeks. We need to be careful when asserting that an entire segment of society has one way of thinking and one way of acting. It can be a slippery slope of over-simplification and cause concerns that hang around the neck of every person in that particular age group.

Many also argue about the ages that pertain to any particular generational classification. If you look at ten different experts on the categorizing of the generations, you'll likely find somewhat differing start and end dates for the age brackets. I won't get into the stickiness of that debate and instead for purposes herein let's just go with some overall age brackets that most seem to agree on.

Here's a rough estimate:
- Baby Boomers: 1946 to 1964
- Gen X (Baby Bust): 1964 to 1975
- Xennials: 1975 to 1985
- Millennials (Gen Y, Gen Next): 1985 to 1995
- Gen Z (iGen): 1995 to 2012
- Gen Alpha: 2013 to 2025

Take a look at Figure 1 for a chart of this generational indication.

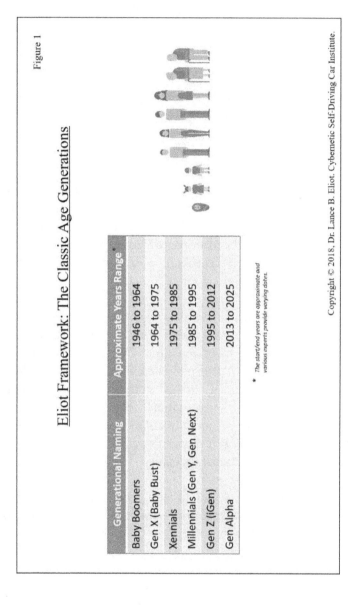

Figure 1

Eliot Framework: The Classic Age Generations

Generational Naming	Approximate Years Range *
Baby Boomers	1946 to 1964
Gen X (Baby Bust)	1964 to 1975
Xennials	1975 to 1985
Millennials (Gen Y, Gen Next)	1985 to 1995
Gen Z (iGen)	1995 to 2012
Gen Alpha	2013 to 2025

* The start/end years are approximate and
various experts provide varying dates.

Should you be interpreting these age brackets in a precise manner? No, heck no. If you were born in 1993, you presumably are a Millennial. But, since you are very close to the end date range of the bracket, one could make the case that perhaps you are more like a Gen Z than a Millennial. If you were born in say 2010, it's kind of a stretch to say that you are a Millennial, and it would likely make more sense to toss in the towel and agree that you are a Gen Z. As I say, though, individual differences make these categories kind of wacky at times.

You might have been raised in a manner that differs from the overall notion of your generation. You might have been raised as suggested by your category, and yet have rebelled or otherwise opted to not conform to the stated nature of your generation. Certainly, your formative years would have been impacted by the events and cultural norms of that time period. It's difficult to extract yourself from the social milieu of a particular time period.

Baby Boomers did not have online social media while growing up. That's a fact. Millennials got the initial tastes of social media and were at the cutting edge. Gen Z has been pretty much steeped in social media and for them it is part-and-parcel of their lives. Some like to refer to the Gen Z as the "digital natives" generation and suggest that they are all about high-tech. They embrace high-tech. Furthermore, they expect high-tech. The prior generations were surprised to see high-tech evolve and emerge. For them, it's an add-on. For the Gen Z, it's a foundation, it's an assumed expectation.

I'm not going to say much herein about the Gen X, the so-called baby bust generation. They are referred to as the "baby bust" because they were a much smaller baby boom than the Baby Boomers generation. The Baby Boomers were spawned by the post-WWII activities of society. Once that tsunami of births ran its course, there was a secondary min-boom of those eldest of the Baby Boomer generation opting to have kids. You've also got the rather small segment known as the Xennials, a kind of now forgotten segment that fits between the Gen X and the Millennials. Few seem to talk about the Xennials as a broad scope of impacting society. Sorry about that, Xennials.

I'd wager a bet that most of the time, whenever there are discussions about generations, it usually consists of the Baby Boomers, the Millennials, and the Gen Z. That's the big three.

Today's news is dominated by the aging of the Baby Boomers and the vast numbers of retirees that we're beginning to experience. All of that massive sized generation is getting to old age. With advances in healthcare and technology, those Baby Boomers are living longer than prior generations. So, you've got them living longer and they are a massive sized group. It's a segment of society to not just wash away because their getting at the end of their careers – don't underestimate the tenacity of those Baby Boomers!

Meanwhile, the Gen Z is picking up speed as it reaches the late teens and starts toward their early 20's. Some refer to them as the iGen. This is due to the popularity of high-tech, whether it be iPhones, iPads, or any kind of "i" that you'd like to use. They are just at the start of the Internet of Things (IoT) advent, and it will be interesting to see how they embrace it (presumably, with both arms wide open and a full embrace).

You've not likely heard much about the Gen Alpha. It's the generation that comes after the Gen Z. Right now, the Gen Alpha is still pretty much in diapers or at most going to elementary school. Plus, a large portion of Gen Alpha doesn't even exist yet. It's going to take Gen Z a few more years to start doing their thing, including starting families, in order to see the population of Gen Alpha take off.

What does all this have to do with AI self-driving cars?

At the Cybernetic AI Self-Driving Car Institute, we are developing AI systems for self-driving cars. When you consider the emergence of AI self-driving cars, it's going to happen during the 2020s, 2030s, and 2040s.

That might seem like an obvious statement, well, of course those AI self-driving cars will emerge over those next three decades. Yes, but have you considered how the advent of AI self-driving cars will coincide with the shifting of the age generations of our society?

I'd bet that you've not yet pondered that aspect.

In the 2020's, the Baby Boomers are going to be less and less involved in the emergence of AI self-driving cars. It makes sense that they would be less involved since they are aging and either nearing retirement or at retirement. They might be quite an audience of people that will use AI self-driving cars, but in terms of developing, refining, testing, and rolling out AI self-driving cars, all that is going to happen once they are no longer in the workforce.

The Millennials will certainly be instrumental in the 2020's and 2030's regarding the fielding of AI self-driving cars. But, many of them will already have defined their careers and be less likely to go whole hog into the AI self-driving car realm. Again, they will be a big-time user of AI self-driving cars. And, they'll be of an age and position to either make troubles for AI self-driving cars or seek to gain acceptance for AI self-driving cars.

The real workhorses for advancing AI self-driving cars is going to fall squarely onto the shoulders of Gen Z.

I'd guess that there's a collective groan coming from many of the Gen Z. What's this, they are responsible now for the fate and future of AI self-driving cars? Don't they already have to contend with global climate change? Don't they already need to be dealing with weapons of mass destruction, or worldwide political turmoil and terrorism. Isn't that already a full plate?

Well, like it or not, want it or not, the fate of AI self-driving cars is going to land on the Gen Z. It's a heavy thing to contend with. I apologize if my mentioning this is going to keep you awake at nights.

I predict that the Gen Z is going to be the generation that either moves us all forward into AI self-driving cars, or for whatever reason decides to delay it, or perhaps even decides to stop it.

Allow me to offer these insights about the Gen Z and the AI self-driving cars fate:

- They say that Gen Z is a much more cautious generation than the Millennials and the Baby Boomers. Will that cautiousness translate into being cautious about the adoption of AI self-driving cars? Will they put on the brakes, so to speak, and not be willing to take gambles on it?

- They say that Gen Z is less optimistic than the prior generations. Will this lessened optimism make them more skeptical and perhaps actually pessimistic about the reality of having true AI self-driving cars? You've got to have some substantive modicum of optimism to believe that AI self-driving cars are really going to happen.

- They say that Gen Z is opting to not buy cars and instead uses and prefers ridsesharing (including that they are foregoing driving). If so, and since AI self-driving cars are predicted to be a boon for ridesharing, maybe the Gen Z will want to not only have AI self-driving cars emerge but be willing to take chances to do so, under the eagerness of shifting us into the mobility-as-an-economy future that many predict we are headed toward.

It's evident that the Gen Z has reasons to want to proceed faithfully and expeditiously on AI self-driving cars. They also though seem to have characteristics that could blunt the movement forward of AI self-driving cars.

There's a definite kind of tension between their presumed wariness, along with their savviness of what high-tech can and cannot do (less chance of being bamboozled, some would say), and their willingness to take chances on something untried and right now still really an experiment.

We've certainly seen generational gaps occur in our society that have involved one generation pushing one agenda, and the next generation perhaps opting to not continue forward on that agenda.

There can be a NIH (Not Invented Here) perspective by a generation that feels a prior generation "stuck" them with something that seems untoward or undesirable. That's a kind of doom-and-gloom version of what the Gen Z might do about AI self-driving cars.

On the other hand, sometimes a next generation decides they can take something that was started by the preceding generation and move it further up the hill. The prior generation is at times thanked for having taken the tough parts of getting stuff underway. The next generation, not exhausted by those initial forays, say that they'll pick-up the mantle and head to the finish line on the effort. They might not even have been tainted by earlier naysayers that said it could not be done. Instead, the next generation rolls easily with the punches and just assumes it can be done.

By the way, that's the happy-face scenario of what Gen Z might do about AI self-driving cars.

When I refer to AI self-driving cars, please be aware that there are various levels of AI self-driving cars. The topmost level is considered Level 5 and consists of a self-driving car that is entirely driven by the AI and there is no human driver involved. Most of the Level 5 self-driving cars lack any brake pedal and nor a gas pedal, and there's not a steering wheel available either. The notion is that the AI is supposed to be the driver and be able to do whatever a human driver could do. Self-driving cars at a less than Level 5 are expected to have a human driver present. The AI co-shares the driving task with the human driver, though this is a dangerous aspect that I continue to warn about.

The reason that I bring up the levels of AI self-driving cars is that the levels less than 5 will be further advancing during the 2020's and 2030s, and the question will loom larger and larger as to how to best co-share the driving task with humans. There are likely to be many incidents in which the human driver assumed the AI was going to handle a driving situation, and yet the AI opted to hand the driving suddenly over to the caught-by-surprise human. Today, the claim is always that the human driver is ultimately responsible, but this is going to increasingly wear thin as a defensive posture on the matter.

Meanwhile, efforts to get to the vaunted Level 5, the truly autonomous AI self-driving car, will likely hit various "roadblocks" too during the 2020s and 2030s. No one can say for sure that we can reach a true Level 5. There are variants of Level 5 that some purists would say are not the "real thing" in terms of what we hope or anticipate a Level 5 self-driving car will be able to do. The efforts to tryout Level 5's on our roadways are likely to introduce untoward incidents and there will be a clamor about whether this public kind of experiment should continue or be modified or possibly curtailed.

Let's consider how Gen Z comes to play in all of this.

Take a look at Figure 2.

Figure 2

Eliot Framework: Gen Z and the Fate of AI Self-Driving Cars

Era	Gen Z (youngest) *	Gen Z (eldest) *	Gen Z (eldest) Life Activities	AI Self-Driving Cars Evolution
2020's	10-20	25-35	Post-college, adulting, career shaping, marriage	AI self-driving cars appearing, crisis of faith in true AI arises, regulations, ethics, etc.
2030's	20-30	35-45	Family start/raising, mid-career, *era responsible*	AI self-driving cars stabilizing, acceptance emerges, key start of growth and prevalence
2040's	30-40	45-55	Key roles in govt and business, setting direction	AI self-driving cars become commonplace, switchover from conventional takes root

The start/end ages are approximate and various experts provide varying indications.

During the 2020s, Gen Z will have its youngest portion in the ages of 10 to 20, which basically means they won't have much to do about the development of AI self-driving cars since they'll be dealing with mainly school. The eldest edge of the Gen Z will be in the mid-20's to mid-30's, a prime time for them of their lives. They are post-college. They are becoming full adults. They are choosing their career paths and starting along those paths. They will undoubtedly shift from a collegiate dating pattern to a more stabilized dating pattern, opting to get married and "settle down" as it were.

They will be in the junior and mid-level ranks of companies. They are tech savvy. Many of them are oriented towards tech related jobs. It's at this time they'll begin to get immersed into the development of AI self-driving cars, taking on what has come before them. They will be faced overall with the potential "crisis in faith" about AI and whether it is really going to achieve the rather high expectations that are being set right now about it. I'd anticipate that the AI mania will begin to subside as people realize the limitations of AI as we know of it today.

On the AI self-driving car front, with various incidents occurring during the 2020s, there is likely to be more stringent regulation coming along. Right now, the regulations are relatively loose, allowing for a latitude of freedom to encourage new innovation in self-driving cars. We are likely though to see this begin to turn in the 2020s. Similar to how Uber and Byrd were able to initially skate along without heavy regulatory requirements, and then it caught up with them, we'll see the same happen to AI self-driving cars. Numerous ethics related questions will also become more apparent to the general public, which otherwise today are only being considered by those in-the-know.

Let's next move into the 2030's. The Gen Z is now starting a family and raising a family. This serious-minded bunch will want to avoid being helicopter parents, and nor will they be convincing their children that they can do anything and be anything. Instead, they'll be introducing them to a world of hard work and facing a myriad of societal and environment problems.

They have now moved into mid-level and higher-level positions, doing so in business and in government.

It is now the time, during the 2030's, a momentous time of the "grand convergence" for the Gen Z, in terms of their personal maturation, their emerging and solidifying position of authority, and the direction and fate of AI self-driving cars becomes inextricably in their hands.

The Gen Z is in-charge of this crucial "tipping point" era of AI self-driving cars. In the 2020's, the Gen Z's were starting to get involved. Now, they are fully involved, and they are ones calling the shots. It is my hope that their serious mindedness and tenacity will get us past the shaky 2020s that had AI self-driving cars on the verge of getting expunged, and instead the Gen Z will find ways to push forward successfully during the 2030s on AI self-driving cars.

If that happens, we'll then enter into the 2040s with the Gen Z now fully having taken ahold of AI self-driving cars (possibly!), and they will have advanced further in their careers. They will be at the tops of companies and the government. Whatever they did in the 2030s, they will now be presumably continuing it and keeping it going. The younger segment of the Gen Z is now the implementers of what the elders of the Gen Z brought to fruition in the 2030s.

Let's also consider what will happen to today's cars by the time we get to the 2030's and 2040s. We currently have around 200+ million conventional cars in the United States alone. I've said many times that these conventional cars are not going to disappear overnight, and nor are they likely to being amenable for conversion into AI self-driving cars. That means we'll have a mix of conventional cars and AI self-driving cars for many years, indeed I'd say many decades. During the 2040s, I would anticipate that the conventional car will finally begin to wane and those that had conventional cars will have given way to instead switching over to AI self-driving cars.

Well, there you have it. Gen Z. Deciders of the future. Fate makers for AI self-driving cars.

They are in the driver's seat when it comes to the future of AI self-driving cars. They probably don't think they are, right now, since they are just starting their lives as the elders of the pack coming into the first difficult moments of their careers. Little do they realize that the maturation of AI self-driving cars is going to coincide with their own maturation. In that sense, they will grow-up together. The question remains whether the Gen Z generation will decide that they like their new brother, or whether they become soured on it. Gen Z, autonomous AI self-driving cars are going to be your hands. Do what's right, thanks!

APPENDIX

APPENDIX A

TEACHING WITH THIS MATERIAL

The material in this book can be readily used either as a supplemental to other content for a class, or it can also be used as a core set of textbook material for a specialized class. Classes where this material is most likely used include any classes at the college or university level that want to augment the class by offering thought provoking and educational essays about AI and self-driving cars.

In particular, here are some aspects for class use:

o   Computer Science. Studying AI, autonomous vehicles, etc.

o   Business. Exploring technology and it adoption for business.

o   Sociology. Sociological views on the adoption and advancement of technology.

Specialized classes at the undergraduate and graduate level can also make use of this material.

For each chapter, consider whether you think the chapter provides material relevant to your course topic. There is plenty of opportunity to get the students thinking about the topic and force them to decide whether they agree or disagree with the points offered and positions taken. I would also encourage you to have the students do additional research beyond the chapter material presented (I provide next some suggested assignments they can do).

RESEARCH ASSIGNMENTS ON THESE TOPICS

Your students can find background material on these topics, doing so in various business and technical publications. I list below the top ranked AI related journals. For business publications, I would suggest the usual culprits such as the Harvard Business Review, Forbes, Fortune, WSJ, and the like.

Here are some suggestions of homework or projects that you could assign to students:

a) <u>Assignment for foundational AI research topic</u>: Research and prepare a paper and a presentation on a specific aspect of Deep AI, Machine Learning, ANN, etc. The paper should cite at least 3 reputable sources. Compare and contrast to what has been stated in this book.

b) <u>Assignment for the Self-Driving Car topic</u>: Research and prepare a paper and Self-Driving Cars. Cite at least 3 reputable sources and analyze the characterizations. Compare and contrast to what has been stated in this book.

c) <u>Assignment for a Business topic</u>: Research and prepare a paper and a presentation on businesses and advanced technology. What is hot, and what is not? Cite at least 3 reputable sources. Compare and contrast to the depictions in this book.

d) <u>Assignment to do a Startup</u>: Have the students prepare a paper about how they might startup a business in this realm. They must submit a sound Business Plan for the startup. They could also be asked to present their Business Plan and so should also have a presentation deck to coincide with it.

You can certainly adjust the aforementioned assignments to fit to your particular needs and the class structure. You'll notice that I ask for 3 reputable cited sources for the paper writing based assignments. I usually steer students toward "reputable" publications, since otherwise they will cite some oddball source that has no credentials other than that they happened to write something and post it onto the Internet. You can define "reputable" in whatever way you prefer, for example some faculty think Wikipedia is not reputable while others believe it is reputable and allow students to cite it.

The reason that I usually ask for at least 3 citations is that if the student only does one or two citations they usually settle on whatever they happened to find the fastest. By requiring three citations, it usually seems to force them to look around, explore, and end-up probably finding five or more, and then whittling it down to 3 that they will actually use.

I have not specified the length of their papers, and leave that to you to tell the students what you prefer. For each of those assignments, you could end-up with a short one to two pager, or you could do a dissertation length paper. Base the length on whatever best fits for your class, and the credit amount of the assignment within the context of the other grading metrics you'll be using for the class.

I mention in the assignments that they are to do a paper and prepare a presentation. I usually try to get students to present their work. This is a good practice for what they will do in the business world. Most of the time, they will be required to prepare an analysis and present it. If you don't have the class time or inclination to have the students present, then you can of course cut out the aspect of them putting together a presentation.

If you want to point students toward highly ranked journals in AI, here's a list of the top journals as reported by *various citation counts sources* (this list changes year to year):

- o   Communications of the ACM
- o   Artificial Intelligence
- o   Cognitive Science
- o   IEEE Transactions on Pattern Analysis and Machine Intelligence
- o   Foundations and Trends in Machine Learning
- o   Journal of Memory and Language
- o   Cognitive Psychology
- o   Neural Networks
- o   IEEE Transactions on Neural Networks and Learning Systems
- o   IEEE Intelligent Systems
- o   Knowledge-based Systems

GUIDE TO USING THE CHAPTERS

For each of the chapters, I provide next some various ways to use the chapter material. You can assign the tasks as individual homework assignments, or the tasks can be used with team projects for the class. You can easily layout a series of assignments, such as indicating that the students are to do item "a" below for say Chapter 1, then "b" for the next chapter of the book, and so on.

a) What is the main point of the chapter and describe in your own words the significance of the topic,

b) Identify at least two aspects in the chapter that you agree with, and support your concurrence by providing at least one other outside researched item as support; make sure to explain your basis for disagreeing with the aspects,

c) Identify at least two aspects in the chapter that you disagree with, and support your disagreement by providing at least one other outside researched item as support; make sure to explain your basis for disagreeing with the aspects,

d) Find an aspect that was not covered in the chapter, doing so by conducting outside research, and then explain how that aspect ties into the chapter and what significance it brings to the topic,

e) Interview a specialist in industry about the topic of the chapter, collect from them their thoughts and opinions, and readdress the chapter by citing your source and how they compared and contrasted to the material,

f) Interview a relevant academic professor or researcher in a college or university about the topic of the chapter, collect from them their thoughts and opinions, and readdress the chapter by citing your source and how they compared and contrasted to the material,

g) Try to update a chapter by finding out the latest on the topic, and ascertain whether the issue or topic has now been solved or whether it is still being addressed, explain what you come up with.

The above are all ways in which you can get the students of your class involved in considering the material of a given chapter. You could mix things up by having one of those above assignments per each week, covering the chapters over the course of the semester or quarter.

As a reminder, here are the chapters of the book and you can select whichever chapters you find most valued for your particular class:

Chapter Title

Companion Book By This Author

Advances in AI and Autonomous Vehicles: Cybernetic Self-Driving Cars

Practical Advances in Artificial Intelligence (AI) and Machine Learning
by
Dr. Lance B. Eliot, MBA, PhD

This title is available via Amazon and other book sellers

Companion Book By This Author

Self-Driving Cars:
"The Mother of All AI Projects"

by Dr. Lance B. Eliot, MBA, PhD

This title is available via Amazon and other book sellers

Companion Book By This Author

Innovation and Thought Leadership
on Self-Driving Driverless Cars

by Dr. Lance B. Eliot, MBA, PhD

This title is available via Amazon and other book sellers

Companion Book By This Author

New Advances in AI Autonomous Driverless Cars Self-Driving Cars

by Dr. Lance B. Eliot, MBA, PhD

Chapter Title

1 Eliot Framework for AI Self-Driving Cars

2 Self-Driving Cars Learning from Self-Driving Cars

3 Imitation as Deep Learning for Self-Driving Cars

4 Assessing Federal Regulations for Self-Driving Cars

5 Bandwagon Effect for Self-Driving Cars

6 AI Backdoor Security Holes for Self-Driving Cars

7 Debiasing of AI for Self-Driving Cars

8 Algorithmic Transparency for Self-Driving Cars

9 Motorcycle Disentanglement for Self-Driving Cars

10 Graceful Degradation Handling of Self-Driving Cars

11 AI for Home Garage Parking of Self-Driving Cars

12 Motivational AI Irrationality for Self-Driving Cars

13 Curiosity as Cognition for Self-Driving Cars

14 Automotive Recalls of Self-Driving Cars

15 Internationalizing AI for Self-Driving Cars

16 Sleeping as AI Mechanism for Self-Driving Cars

17 Car Insurance Scams and Self-Driving Cars

18 U-Turn Traversal AI for Self-Driving Cars

19 Software Neglect for Self-Driving Cars

This title is available via Amazon and other book sellers

Companion Book By This Author

Introduction to
Driverless Self-Driving Cars

by Dr. Lance B. Eliot, MBA, PhD

Chapter Title

This title is available via Amazon and other book sellers

Companion Book By This Author
Autonomous Vehicle Driverless
Self-Driving Cars and Artificial Intelligence
by Dr. Lance B. Eliot, MBA, PhD

This title is available via Amazon and other book sellers

Companion Book By This Author

Transformative Artificial Intelligence Driverless Self-Driving Cars

by Dr. Lance B. Eliot, MBA, PhD

This title is available via Amazon and other book sellers

Companion Book By This Author

Disruptive Artificial Intelligence and Driverless Self-Driving Cars

by Dr. Lance B. Eliot, MBA, PhD

This title is available via Amazon and other book sellers

Companion Book By This Author

State-of-the-Art
AI Driverless Self-Driving Cars

by Dr. Lance B. Eliot, MBA, PhD

This title is available via Amazon and other book sellers

Companion Book By This Author

Top Trends in
AI Self-Driving Cars

by Dr. Lance B. Eliot, MBA, PhD

Chapter Title

This title is available via Amazon and other book sellers

Companion Book By This Author

AI Innovations and Self-Driving Cars

by Dr. Lance B. Eliot, MBA, PhD

Chapter Title

This title is available via Amazon and other book sellers

Companion Book By This Author

Crucial Advances for AI Self-Driving Cars

by Dr. Lance B. Eliot, MBA, PhD

This title is available via Amazon and other book sellers

<u>Companion Book By This Author</u>

Sociotechnical Insights and AI Self-Driving Cars

by Dr. Lance B. Eliot, MBA, PhD

<u>Chapter Title</u>

This title is available via Amazon and other book sellers

ABOUT THE AUTHOR

Dr. Lance B. Eliot, MBA, PhD is the CEO of Techbruim, Inc. and Executive Director of the Cybernetic Self-Driving Car Institute, and has over twenty years of industry experience including serving as a corporate officer in a billion dollar firm and was a partner in a major executive services firm. He is also a serial entrepreneur having founded, ran, and sold several high-tech related businesses. He previously hosted the popular radio show *Technotrends* that was also available on American Airlines flights via their in-flight audio program. Author or co-author of a dozen books and over 400 articles, he has made appearances on CNN, and has been a frequent speaker at industry conferences.

A former professor at the University of Southern California (USC), he founded and led an innovative research lab on Artificial Intelligence in Business. Known as the "AI Insider" his writings on AI advances and trends has been widely read and cited. He also previously served on the faculty of the University of California Los Angeles (UCLA), and was a visiting professor at other major universities. He was elected to the International Board of the Society for Information Management (SIM), a prestigious association of over 3,000 high-tech executives worldwide.

He has performed extensive community service, including serving as Senior Science Adviser to the Vice Chair of the Congressional Committee on Science & Technology. He has served on the Board of the OC Science & Engineering Fair (OCSEF), where he is also has been a Grand Sweepstakes judge, and likewise served as a judge for the Intel International SEF (ISEF). He served as the Vice Chair of the Association for Computing Machinery (ACM) Chapter, a prestigious association of computer scientists. Dr. Eliot has been a shark tank judge for the USC Mark Stevens Center for Innovation on start-up pitch competitions, and served as a mentor for several incubators and accelerators in Silicon Valley and Silicon Beach. He served on several Boards and Committees at USC, including having served on the Marshall Alumni Association (MAA) Board in Southern California.

Dr. Eliot holds a PhD from USC, MBA, and Bachelor's in Computer Science, and earned the CDP, CCP, CSP, CDE, and CISA certifications. Born and raised in Southern California, and having traveled and lived internationally, he enjoys scuba diving, surfing, and sailing.

ADDENDUM

Pioneering Advances for AI Driverless Cars

Practical Advances in Artificial Intelligence (AI) and Machine Learning

By

Dr. Lance B. Eliot, MBA, PhD

For supplemental materials of this book, visit:

www.ai-selfdriving-cars.guru

For special orders of this book, contact:

LBE Press Publishing

Email: LBE.Press.Publishing@gmail.com

www.ingramcontent.com/pod-product-compliance
Lightning Source LLC
Chambersburg PA
CBHW051229050326
40689CB00007B/848